The Book of Horsemanship

By Duarte I of Portugal

Armour and Weapons

ISSN 1746-9449

Series Editors

Kelly DeVries
Robert W. Jones
Robert C. Woosnam-Savage

Throughout history armour and weapons have been not merely the preserve of the warrior in battles and warfare, but potent symbols in their own right (the sword of chivalry, the heraldic shield) representing the hunt and hall as well as the battlefield. This series aims to provide a forum for critical studies of all aspects of arms and armour and their technologies, from the end of the Roman Empire to the dawn of the modern world; both new research and works of synthesis are encouraged.

New proposals for the series are welcomed; they should be sent to the publisher at the address below.

Boydell & Brewer Limited, PO Box 9, Woodbridge, Suffolk, IP12 3DF

Previously published titles in the series are listed at the back of this volume

The Book of Horsemanship
By Duarte I of Portugal

Translated by
Jeffrey L. Forgeng

THE BOYDELL PRESS

Translation and editorial matter © Jeffrey L. Forgeng 2016

All rights reserved. Except as permitted under current legislation no part of this work may be photocopied, stored in a retrieval system, published, performed in public, adapted, broadcast, transmitted, recorded or reproduced in any form or by any means, without the prior permission of the copyright owner

The right of Jeffrey L. Forgeng to be identified as the author of this work has been asserted in accordance with sections 77 and 78 of the Copyright, Designs and Patents Act 1988

First published 2016
Paperback edition 2023

The Boydell Press, Woodbridge

ISBN 978 1 78327 103 0 hardback
ISBN 978 1 83765 107 8 paperback

The Boydell Press is an imprint of Boydell & Brewer Ltd
PO Box 9, Woodbridge, Suffolk IP12 3DF, UK
and of Boydell & Brewer Inc.
668 Mt Hope Avenue, Rochester, NY 14620–2731, USA
website: www.boydellandbrewer.com

A CIP catalogue record for this book is available
from the British Library

The publisher has no responsibility for the continued existence or accuracy of URLs for external or third-party internet websites referred to in this book, and does not guarantee that any content on such websites is, or will remain, accurate or appropriate

Contents

List of Plates	vi
Acknowledgements	vii
Introduction	1
Duarte I	3
The *Livro do Cavalgar*	9
Duarte and Equestrian Literature	13
Medieval Horses and Equestrianism	17
Tack	18
Bits and Bridles	22
Spurs	26
Riding	27
Lanceplay	30
Duarte and the Horse	32
The *Livro do Cavalgar* and Other Technical Domains	34
Note on the Translation	45
***The Book of Horsemanship* by Duarte I of Portugal**	47
[Prologue]	47
Here begins Part I of this book, which deals with the Will	50
Here ends Part I, concerning the Will, and begins Part II, concerning Ability	54
Part III, offering Sixteen Chief Recommendations for the good rider	56
Bibliography	155
Manuscripts	155
Editions and Translations of Duarte's Works	155
Other Printed Works	156
Index	171

Plates

Plate 1. The opening of the *Livro do Cavalgar* (Paris, Bibliothèque Nationale MS portuguais 5, fol. 99r). — 10

Plate 2. A pack-saddle, 1502 (Munich, Bayerische Staatsbibliothek Cod. icon. 222, fol. 23v). — 19

Plate 3. A horse with war saddle, c. 1460 (Biblioteca Apostolica Vaticana MS Ott. lat. 1417, fol. 22r). — 21

Plate 4. Sketch of a horse wearing a curb bit, by Antonio Pisanello, mid-1400s (Musée du Louvre, Inv. 2359, Recto, Fonds des dessins et miniatures). — 24

Plate 5. Rowel spur, c. 1400. Worcester Art Museum (MA), The John Woodman Higgins Collection, 2014.991. Image © Worcester Art Museum, All Rights Reserved. — 27

Plate 6. Christians and Moors in battle, from the *Altarpiece of St. George*, c. 1420s (Victoria and Albert Museum 1217–1864). — 28

Plate 7. A rider and horse equipped for jousting, 1460s (Vienna, Österreichische Nationalbibliothek, Codex Vindobonensis 2597, fol. 5v). — 31

Plate 8. A joust of peace, 1480s (British Library, MS Cotton Julius E IV, fol. 15v). — 37

Plate 9. Lance-tip of coronel form, early 1500s. Worcester Art Museum (MA), The John Woodman Higgins Collection, 2014.668. — 38

Plate 10. "Stirrups", plate 9 from the series *Nova Reperta* (New Discoveries), Theodor Galle, about 1570–1633, after Johannes Stradanus (Flemish, 1523–1605), about 1580. Worcester Art Museum (MA), 2006.9. Image © Worcester Art Museum, All Rights Reserved. — 40

The author and publishers are grateful to all the institutions and individuals listed for permission to reproduce the materials in which they own copyright. Every effort has been made to trace the copyright holders; apologies are offered for any omission and the publishers will be pleased to add any necessary acknowledgment in subsequent editions

Acknowledgements

Dom Duarte's treatise on horsemanship is a complex work touching on a wide variety of disciplines, and this book would not have been possible without drawing on the expertise of a number of people. I would like to thank Jennifer and Robert Reed for their tireless assistance with multiple aspects of this work, and indeed for the copy of Piel's edition that launched this project in the first place. I am also grateful for invaluable guidance on equestrian matters from Patrice Edwards, Jeffrey Hedgecock, and Arne Koets. Thanks are likewise due to Krista Baker for her insights on throwing sports and to Gwen Nowrick for her expertise on fifteenth-century costume. I would particularly like to thank Robert Macpherson for his detailed and characteristically perceptive insights on draft versions of the work, and Aarti Madan for helping me extricate myself from an especially glutinous passage in the Portuguese. I also owe thanks to Tobias Capwell for sharing his extraordinary knowledge of medieval equestrianism and equestrian sports. I would like to thank Joseph Suárez for his assistance in covering the cost of permissions for the illustrations. Lastly, but most importantly, I would like to thank Noel Fallows for a level of assistance that can hardly be overestimated. This work was for a long time intended for publication as part of a collaborative volume involving the two of us and three Iberian chivalric texts. For practical reasons the project had to be reconfigured, but in the mean time Prof. Fallows provided extensive and invaluable assistance without which this volume would have been immeasurably the poorer.

Introduction

> I would have our Courtier be a perfect horseman in every kind of saddle; and in addition to knowing about horses and what pertains to a horseman, let him put every effort and diligence into surpassing others a little in everything. ... As it is the peculiar excellence of the Italians to ride well in the brida style, to practice manège skillfully, especially with challenging horses, to tilt and joust, let him be among the best of the Italians in this. In tourneying, conducting a deed of arms, fighting at the barriers, let him be among the best of the French. In cane games, bullfighting, throwing spears and javelins, let him be outstanding among the Spaniards.
> —Baldesar Castiglione, *The Book of the Courtier*, Book I ch. 21[1]

In 1804, the Portuguese abbot, diplomat, and scholar José Correia da Serra was residing in Paris, having been obliged two years earlier to resign from his position at the Portuguese embassy in London owing to conflicts with the ambassador. Taking advantage of the opportunity to visit the Bibliothèque Nationale—formerly the French Royal Library, now owned by the nation in Napoleonic France—Correia da Serra came upon a four hundred-year old manuscript from his native land. It turned out to consist of two works by Duarte I of Portugal (r. 1433–1438), *Leal Conselheiro* ("the Faithful Counselor") and the *Livro do Cavalgar* ("Book on Riding").[2] Duarte was known to Portuguese historians as a scholarly monarch, but until this time his reputation rested heavily on references in medieval Portuguese

---

[1] Castiglione, *Il Cortegiano*, fols 17v–18r.
[2] The manuscript does not title the work, but describes it as *o livro da enssynança de bem cavalgar toda sela que fez Elrrey dom Eduarte* ("the book of instruction for riding well in every type of saddle written by the king Dom Duarte"). The catalogue of Duarte's library styles it the *livro do cavalgar que el rey dom Eduarte copilou* (see below, p. 9). *Livro do Cavalgar* may therefore serve as a suitable title, here rendered as *Book of Horsemanship*.

chronicles, since no copy of either of his two major works was known to have survived.

Correia da Serra never publicized his discovery; the manuscript was rediscovered about a decade later, and not until 1843 were its contents finally published. The texts have since been republished several times, but more than two centuries after their discovery, neither one has been made available in a viable English translation.[3] The lack of attention to Duarte outside of Portugal reflects the underdeveloped state of Portuguese studies in the English-speaking world rather than the merits of his work: Duarte is among the most strikingly original authors of the Middle Ages, and had these works been composed by a Spanish or French monarch, they would assuredly be quite familiar to English-speaking scholars.

Students of medieval chivalric culture have reason to be thankful that Duarte turned his sharp intellect to the subject of horsemanship. Modern imagination may associate knights chiefly with swords and armor, but contemporaries knew that the horse was at least as important in the material culture of chivalry. In most western European languages, the word for "knight" is some variant on "horseman", and boys of knightly class trained on horseback years before they were ready to bear arms. As the thirteenth-century veterinary author Jordanus Ruffus expresses it, "The horse separates princes, magnates, and knights from lesser people, and no lord can fittingly be seen among ordinary people except through the mediation of a horse."[4] Yet technical documentation of the equestrian arts of the medieval knight is almost entirely lacking. Prior to Duarte, the only work on the subject in the western tradition is the treatise by Xenophon, composed around the mid-300s B.C.E. A bit more than a century after Duarte, Federico Grisone published his highly influential work on the topic; only after Grisone does material on the subject become plentiful. Duarte stands as the sole medieval writer to provide extensive documentation on what might be considered a knight's most fundamental professional skill—and in terms that still had relevance a hundred years later, as witnessed by Castiglione's recommendations in *The Courtier*.

---

[3] See below, The Translation, on editions and translations of the *Livro do Cavalgar*.
[4] *Jordani Ruffi Calabriensis Hippiatria*, p. 1.

Duarte I

Eduarte I of Portugal (Duarte as he is known in modern Portuguese) was born on 31 October 1391, the second son of João I (1358–1433), founder of the house of Avis that would rule Portugal until 1580. João, a bastard son of Pedro I (r. 1357–1367), was chosen for the throne in 1385 by the Portuguese *cortes* (parliament) after a two-year crisis at the death of João's half-brother Fernando I (r. 1367–1383). The rival claimant was Fernando's sister Beatriz: since she was married to Juan I of Castile, her succession would have meant the end of Portugal as an independent kingdom. Shortly after his accession, João defeated an invading force from Castile with the aid of allied English troops; in 1387, he consolidated his alliance with Richard II of England by marrying Philippa of Lancaster (1359–1415), the daughter of Richard's uncle John of Gaunt. The couple's first son, Afonso, was born in 1390, but died in childhood. Their second son, Duarte, was named after Philippa's grandfather, Edward III of England. Duarte's younger brothers were Pedro (b. 1392), Enrique (b. 1394), João (b. 1400), and Fernando (b. 1402); he also had a sister Isabella (b. 1397), as well as an illegitimate half-brother Afonso (b. 1377) and half-sister Beatriz (b. c. 1386).[5]

Even though Duarte was heir apparent, there is surprisingly little documentation about his first two decades of life. One detail of potential significance to the present work lies in a letter of João I from 1405 mentioning a journey by the princes to England[6]—João does not specify which of his sons were traveling, but the letter may indicate that Duarte visited his mother's homeland at least once, and that his remarks on English riders (III.1 ch. 3), and perhaps those on Irish riders (III.6 ch. 1), were based on experiences abroad.

In 1411, João resolved to undertake an attack on the Moroccan port of Ceuta, at the eastern end of the Strait of Gibraltar. During the following years, as he turned his attention to the preparations for the expedition, he delegated the workings of daily government to

---

[5] On Duarte's siblings, see Lopes, *Chronica de El-Rei D. João I*, 6.85–87.
[6] Dinis, *Monumenta Henricina*, 1.311.

Duarte.[7] The burdens of state proved overwhelming for the young prince, who sank into a paralyzing depression for the next three years. In *Leal Conselheiro* Duarte offers a remarkable narrative and analysis of his depression, applying to it much of the same freshness of insight that makes his *Livro do Cavalgar* speak across the centuries:

> **Chapter 19: How I suffered from melancholic humor and recovered from it**
>
> Many people have been, are, and in the future will be afflicted with this sin of sadness that arises from the disconcerted will, which these days is usually diagnosed as suffering from melancholic humor; physicians say it can arise in many ways due to diverse causes and feelings. For more than three years I was continually and greatly afflicted by it, and by the special grace of our Lord God I returned to perfect health. In pursuit of the intention I expressed at the outset, to offer people beneficial instruction and guidance from this brief and simple reading, I will describe for you the onset, course, and cure of my ailment, so that my experience can be an example for others. For it is no small comfort and remedy to those who are so afflicted to know that others have felt what they are suffering, and have regained complete health: one of its greatest symptoms is the belief, when you are feeling something so terrible, that you can never return to the good condition you were in before.[8]

The episode may have played an important role in the genesis of the *Livro do Cavalgar*. Duarte attributes the onset of his depression in part to a lack of recreation, especially hunting, and recalls that "sadness began to grow in me, not from any real basis, but from anything that might give it occasion, or from any irrational fantasy".[9] This analysis of the causes of his depression brings additional meaning to his rationale for the *Livro do Cavalgar*: in the Prologue, Duarte says that one purpose of writing was "to keep my mind from

---

[7] Gama, *A filosofia da cultura portuguesa*, p. 53; Luis Miguel Duarte, *D. Duarte*, pp. 49, 62.
[8] Duarte, *Leal Conselheiro*, ed. Lopes de Castro and Botelho, p. 73. For the full narrative, see Duarte, *Leal Conselheiro*, pp. 73–83 (chs. 18–25). The episode is also referenced by Zurara, *Tomada de Ceuta*, p. 89.
[9] Duarte, *Leal Conselheiro*, p. 74.

matters that might lead to trouble". Taken together, these passages suggest that the work may have had a place in the author's regime of mental health, offering a vehicle to occupy his mind during idle moments, diverting it from the melancholic thoughts that could lead to depression.

By the time João's fleet was ready to sail in July 1415, the prince had recovered from his depression, and he joined his father and two oldest brothers in the expedition; all three princes took an active part in the fighting. The city fell to the Portuguese on 14 August, an event that marked an important milestone in the establishment of Portugal's global maritime empire. Duarte's experience on this expedition certainly informs his discussion of the role of horsemanship in battle, where he makes particular reference to his father's campaigns (I ch. 1). It may also have influenced his discussion of the riding styles of the Moors (III.1 ch. 7, III.6 ch. 1), though he would also have had occasion to see this at home, where both resident and visiting Moors were a familiar sight.[10]

During the period after Ceuta, the crown prince continued to play an important part in his father's government, but he evidently had sufficient time for a balanced repertoire of physical and intellectual pursuits. In 1421, Alonso de Cartagena, Dean of Santiago de Compostela, arrived from the court of Castile for the first of four diplomatic missions that would eventually culminate in the Peace of Medina del Campo between Castile and Portugal in 1431. Cartagena, who would serve as one of the Castilian delegates to the Council of Basel in the 1430s, was one of Iberia's leading scholars, and he and Duarte appear to have quickly developed a close intellectual bond. Cartagena dedicated to Duarte his *Memoriale Virtutum*, a digest of Aristotle's *Nichomachean Ethics* as expounded by Thomas Aquinas, and it is highly probable that Cartagena was personally responsible for the Aristotelian influences that figure so prominently in the *Livro*

---

[10] On the presence of Moors among the royal stablemasters, see Gomes, *Court Society*, p. 192; on Moorish ambassadors, see Zurara, *Tomada de Ceuta*, p. 105. See also Marques, *Portugal na Crise*, pp. 33–35 on Moors in fifteenth-century Portugal. On Duarte's participation in the fighting at Ceuta, see Zurara, *Tomada de Ceuta*, pp. 196, 203–12, 231–32, 250–53.

do Cavalgar.¹¹ This period also appears to have been the most fruitful for Duarte's own writing, being the likely time for the composition of the *Livro do Cavalgar* and *Leal Conselheiro*, both of which appear to have been composed over a span of years.

As crown prince, Duarte was naturally expected to ensure the continuance of the royal line, though in fact he did not marry until 1428, surprisingly late in life. His wife was Eleanor, daughter of King Ferdinand I of Aragon, and the couple would have nine children during their decade of marriage, though Duarte's first child, João Manuel de Vilhena, was born out of wedlock around 1416. The bond between Duarte and Eleanor seems to have been very real, as evidenced by his dedication of *Leal Conselheiro* to his wife, and the apparent creation of a presentation copy of both of Duarte's major works for her.

In the latter years of João I's reign, the crown prince was playing an increasing role in his father's government, and by the time he acceded to the throne in 1433, Duarte was already an experienced ruler. His actual reign was brief, and was not judged favorably either by contemporaries or subsequent generations, owing to a disastrous attempt to seize Tangier in 1437: the attack failed, and the king's youngest brother was captured, to die in captivity a few years later. Recent scholarship is less inclined to judge Duarte's reign purely by his military record. His administration was diligent and able, both as prince and as king: his legacy included substantial development of the law code as well as currency reform. Perhaps most significantly, he left behind him a nation remarkably stable, in spite of dynastic conflicts in both the preceding and following generations, positioning Portugal to play a global role that no contemporary could have anticipated based on the country's size, population, or wealth.¹²

Duarte succumbed to the plague only a year after Tangier, dying on 9 September 1438. His six-year old son succeeded to the throne

---

[11] Fallows, "Alfonso de Cartagena", pp. 6–7; Cartagena, *Memorial de Virtudes*, ed. Campos Souto, pp. 15–16, 29–30, 34–35; Gallardo, *Alonso de Cartagena*, pp. 119–25; Salazar, "Impacto Humanístico", pp. 219–24.

[12] For modern interpretations of Duarte, cf. Dionísio, "Recepção de D. Duarte"; Gama, *Filosofia da cultura portuguesa*, pp. 53–54; Russell, *Prince Henry*, 149–50; Marques, *Portugal na Crise*, pp. 548–42. For examples of some of Duarte's governmental work, see Albuquerque and Nunes, *Ordenações del-Rei Dom Duarte*; Marques, *Portugal na Crise*, pp. 211, 281.

as Afonso V. At first the boy ruled under the regency of his mother, but after a period of conflict between Eleanor and her brother-in-law Pedro, she left the country in 1440 to settle in Toledo. The House of Avis would continue to oversee Portugal's emergence onto the world stage, until the death of the last Avis king in 1580 resulted in a period of rule by the kings of Spain until the mid-1600s.[13]

About sixty years after Duarte's death, the Portuguese court historian Rui de Pina described him in terms predictably flattering, but generally consistent with external evidence:

> He was an agile man, and well trained in all the good arts that an accomplished prince should possess in field and court, peace and war. He knew how to ride in both brida and jennet saddles better than anyone else in his day; he was very kind to everyone, and well tempered; he prided himself on being a good wrestler in his youth, as indeed he was, and he often practiced with contemporaries who were also good at it; he enjoyed hunting large and small game, although not at the cost of falling behind on necessary business. ... He was a wise man and possessed of a keen intellect, a lover of learning, in which he was very well versed, not so much through attending school, but through ongoing study and reading good books—for his formal studies had been limited to grammar and some logic. He wrote a book of instructions for riders; and he composed another, dedicated to his wife, entitled *Leal Conselheiro*.[14]

Today, Duarte is known to the Portuguese as "the philosopher-king" or "the eloquent", a reputation that rests largely on his surviving writings. His literary output was exceptional among medieval monarchs, but less so within his immediate family. As Duarte mentions in the present work, his father composed a treatise on hunting, the *Livro da Montaria*, written at some point between 1415 and 1433.[15] João's work is several times the size of Duarte's *Livro do Cavalgar*, but otherwise there are pronounced familial resemblances: João integrates psychological, philosophical and ethical reflections

---

[13] On Duarte's life and reign, see Luis Miguel Duarte, *D. Duarte*; Rui de Pina, *Crónicas*, 475–575; Zurara, *Tomada de Ceuta*.
[14] Pina, *Crónicas*, pp. 494–95.
[15] João I, *Montaria*, pp. xxii–xxiii.

with extremely precise detail on the equipment, techniques, and strategies of the hunt. His treatise on hunting was almost certainly a major inspiration for his son, as suggested by repeated references to the late king in the *Livro do Cavalgar* (III.5 ch. 11; III.5 ch 14).

Duarte's brother Pedro likewise had a scholarly bent. He commissioned or authored translations of several classical works—Rui de Pina tells us that his translations included the *De Re Militari* by Vegetius and the *De Regimine Principum* by Giles of Rome, both works that are referenced in the *Livro do Cavalgar*. Pedro also collaborated with the priest João Verba in authoring the *Livro da Virtuosa Bemfeitoria*, an analysis of the dynamics and implications of giving and receiving based on Pedro's translation of Seneca's *De Beneficiis*.[16]

Duarte's own literary output was extensive, if fragmented. In addition to the *Livro do Cavalgar*, he left behind a body of poetry, letters, legal texts, and memoranda on topics as diverse as personal biography, translation theory, customs rates, engineering, and household management.[17] Some of these materials found their way into *Leal Conseilhero*, his most substantial work, a compendium whose subject-matter ranges from philosophy, ethics, and psychology, to such practical matters as diet, timekeeping, and management of the royal chapel.[18] Some of the chapters are copied, adapted, or translated from other sources, including three chapters from the *Livro do Cavalgar*:

Leal Conseilhero	*Livro do Cavalgar*
Ch. 3	III.5 ch. 8
Ch. 5	III.5 ch. 9
Ch. 83	III.1 ch. 11

---

[16] Pedro, Infante of Portugal, and Fr. João Verba, *Livro da Vertuosa Benfeytoria*, ed. Adelino de Almeida Calado, esp. p. ix; Pedro, Infante of Portugal, *Livro dos Ofícios*; Greenfield, "The Patrimonial State"; Dias, *Arte de Ser Bom Cavaleiro*, p. 12; Salazar, "Impacto Humanistico", pp. 224–25. On the family's literary works in general, see Bell, *Portuguese Literature*, pp. 89–92; Gavilanes Laso, "La prosa profana", pp. 135–45; Lapa, *Dom Duarte e os Prosadores da Casa de Avis*. Cf. also below, p. 136 fn. 30.

[17] See Duarte, *Livro dos Conselhos*.

[18] On Duarte's works, see Botelho, *D. Duarte*; Lapa, "D. Duarte e a Prosa Didactica".

The *Livro do Cavalgar*

The *Livro do Cavalgar* survives in only a single copy, Paris Bibliothèque Nationale MS portuguais 5 (formerly MS 7007 of the French Royal Library), fols 99r–128r. The manuscript was not created before 1437, based on references to Duarte as king, and almost certainly not after 1440, when it appears to have left Portugal in the hands of Queen Eleanor. The codex is in folio format, unillustrated but richly adorned with decorative initials and marginal embellishments. The only other text in the manuscript is the sole surviving copy of Duarte's *Leal Conselheiro*, a work dedicated to Queen Eleanor: given the sumptuousness of the manuscript and what can be documented of its history, it may well have been commissioned for the queen.

A list of the contents of Duarte's library, compiled during his reign, includes a "book on riding composed by the king Dom Eduarte", certainly the same work, though perhaps not the same copy.[19] The work is also mentioned around 1500 in Rui de Pina's biography of Duarte. The passage, cited above, suggests that the author might actually have seen a copy of the work. About a hundred years later the *Livro do Cavalgar* is referenced by Duarte Nunes de Leão in his *Crónicas*, in terms that suggest that he had never actually seen it: "He composed a book for horsemen, in which he apparently gave instructions for riding well and for governing horses."[20] At about the same time the book was mentioned by Bernardo de Brito in his *Elógios dos Reis de Portugal*; both Brito and Leão are heavily dependent on Pina, and may simply be embroidering on their source. Manuel Carlos Andrade's 1790 treatise on horsemanship mentions the work, dating it to 1435, but referencing content that is not actually in the text, suggesting that Andrade had access to some other old book on horsemanship and wrongly identified it with Duarte's treatise.[21]

---

[19] Duarte, *Livro dos Conselhos*, p. 208.
[20] Leão, *Crónica*, pp. 778–79.
[21] Andrade, *Arte da cavallaria*, pp. 14, 339–40. In the latter passage, Andrade tell us that on p. 179 of Duarte's book the author recommends "placing the horse between two pillars using a headstall that I have invented". See also Pereira, *Naissance et Renaissance*, pp. 58–60. For other early references to Duarte's work, see Bourdon, "Question de priorité", pp. 4–7.

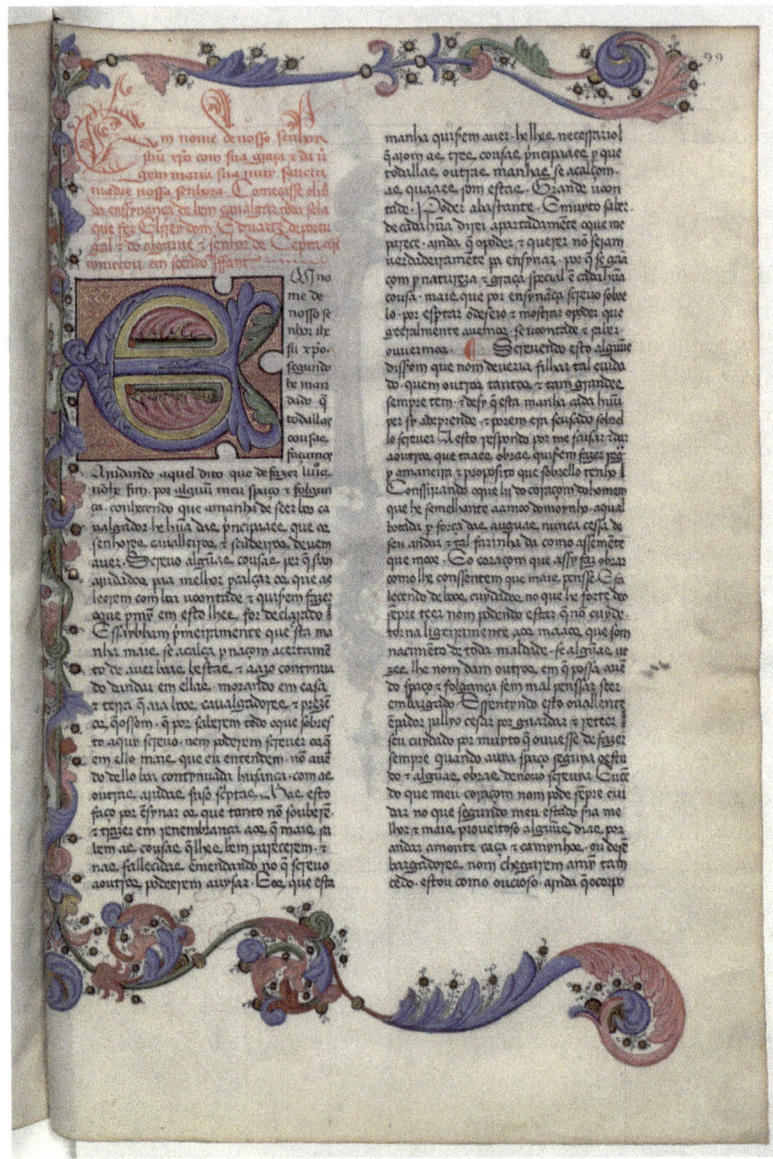

Plate 1. The opening of the *Livro do Cavalgar*
(Paris, Bibliothèque Nationale MS portuguais 5, fol. 99r).

Since the work was never finished, there may never have been more than two copies: Duarte's working version and a copy made for Eleanor. The latter appears to have left Portugal with her in 1440; Duarte's working copy was lost, and by 1600 the text was known to Duarte's countrymen only from written references. The surviving manuscript probably passed from Eleanor to her brother Alfonso V of Aragon, who began assembling a major royal library in 1442, at the time of his conquest of Naples. The codex was certainly in the library of Alfonso's son Fernando I in Naples during the late 1400s, a fact attested to by the shelfmark found on the final page of the text (fol. 128r).[22] The French king Charles VIII in turn conquered Naples in 1495: the manuscript may have been transported to France at this time as part of the captured Neapolitan royal library, or it may have been purchased from Isabelle de Baux, widow of Federigo III, the last Aragonese king of Naples, who sold parts of the library to Louis XII in the early 1500s. The manuscript is listed in several inventories of the French royal library from 1544 onward, invariably mentioning only *Leal Conseilhero*, which suggests that the contents were only superficially examined.[23]

The royal library ultimately became the basis for the Bibliothèque Nationale, where Correia da Serra found the manuscript in 1804. The abbot transcribed the texts, but never published his discovery, and in 1820 the soldier and statesman José Xavier Días da Silva published the first notice of the manuscript, which he had evidently discovered on his own during the previous decade while living as an exile in Paris. The contents of the manuscript were finally printed in two almost simultaneous editions of 1843 in Lisbon and Paris.[24] The standard modern edition was produced by the Lorrainian philologist Joseph Piel in 1944.[25]

---

[22] Castro, "Leal Conseilheiro", pp. 116–18; Dias, *Arte de Ser Bom Cavaleiro*, pp. 45–46.
[23] Castro, "Leal Conseilheiro", pp. 118–19; Dias, *Arte de Ser Bom Cavaleiro*, pp. 43–45.
[24] Bourdon, "Question de priorité"; Castro, "Leal Conseilheiro," p. 110; Castro, *Leal conselheiro*, pp. xvii–xxi; Dias, *Arte de Ser Bom Cavaleiro*, p. 42.
[25] On the history of scholarship on the text, see Bourdon, "Question de priorité"; Maués, "As ensinanças do livro do cavalgar", pp. 208–16.

The bulk of the text was written before Duarte became king, as indicated by the introductory comments in the Prologue and in III.6. Only III.6 and III.7 were written after Duarte's accession in 1433; the reference to a four-year hiatus (III.6 ch. 1) suggests that they were written around the final year of Duarte's life. There was also some revision of the pre-1433 material after Duarte's accession: the first sentence of the Prologue, as well as periodic references to the late king, must have taken their existing form during Duarte's reign.[26]

The structure of Duarte's book is clear in the author's mind, but may not be immediately evident to the reader.[27] His overall organizational scheme is embedded in the Prologue, where he lists the properties needed in order to acquire the art of horsemanship: will, ability, and knowledge. These correspond to the three main divisions of the book:

> Part I: Reasons why one should want to learn horsemanship (Will)
> Part II: Reasons why anyone can become a good horseman (Ability)
> Part III: Skills essential to a good horseman (Knowledge)

The first two parts are brief, serving as a preamble to the main matter of the book in Part III. Part III begins with a list that serves as a guide to the planned structure of the remainder of the work, enumerating sixteen areas of skill required for good horsemanship. These sixteen rubrics are intended as organizational divisions for the rest of the work, although as the following list indicates, some sections stray considerably from the main topic (a fact Duarte himself acknowledges at various points in the text—cf. III.1 ch. 11, III.5 chs. 8, 9, 16), and only the topics in boldface are actually covered.

1. **Strength**, including equipment, styles of riding, wrestling on horseback
2. **Fearlessness**
3. **Confidence**
4. **Steadiness**

---

[26] On the date, see also Dias, *Arte de Ser Bom Cavaleiro*, pp. 49–50.
[27] On the structure of the text, see also Dias, *Arte de Ser Bom Cavaleiro*, pp. 50–55.

5. **Fluidity** (*soltura*), including use of the spear and sword, throwing, jousting, and wrestling on foot
6. **Use of the spurs and rod**
7. The contact between the rider's hand and the horse's mouth through the reins and bit
8. **Hazards** (written as Section 7)
9. Terrain
10. Judiciousness
11. Elegance
12. Endurance
13. Horses' mouths and bits
14. Dealing with horses' faults[28]
15. Fostering horses' virtues
16. Evaluating horses

Duarte evidently planned to cover each of these topics in succession. Topics 1–5 correspond to Sections 1–5 of Part III, the portions completed by 1433. Around 1437, Duarte picked up the project again, writing in a very condensed fashion to cover topics 6 and 8; the final section rushes almost breathlessly through the subject-matter. Even as late as the final page Duarte still envisioned adding more material to the book than he was able to complete before his death (III.6 ch. 2, III.7), and the text breaks off without any sense of closure even of the chapter—the concluding *Deo gracias* probably comes from the scribe rather than the author.

Duarte and Equestrian Literature

In the Prologue, Duarte expresses his pleasure at being the first person to write on the subject of horsemanship. Among European authors of surviving works, that distinction actually belongs to Xenophon, whose *Horsemanship*, composed c. 375–350 B.C.E., offers a brief but technically specific discussion of the techniques of training and riding horses. Nonetheless, Duarte is the only author from the medieval

---

[28] Duarte's intended content for this section may be compared to Grisone, *Rules of Riding*, pp. 293–313.

West to have addressed the subject in detail.²⁹ The closest parallels prior to 1500 are to be found in the *Collectanea* of the Spanish knight Pietro Monte, published in 1509, but based on materials composed around 1490, and related to matter published in Monte's *De Dignoscendis Hominibus* of 1492. Monte's work focuses on the skills and knowledge required of a knight, including a significant amount of material relating to horsemanship. As the following pages will suggest, the *Collectanea* overlaps with the *Livro do Cavalgar* in mindset as well as subject matter, possibly reflecting a shared Iberian tradition of thinking about these physical practices.³⁰ Not until the 1500s does a significant European corpus of writings on equestrianism appear, beginning particularly with the publication of Federico Grisone's

---

[29] Medieval Islamic literature on the subject appears earlier and in greater abundance; see al-Sarraf, "Close Combat Weapons"; Ibn Hudhayl, *La parure des chevaliers*, transl. Mercier, pp. 141–57, 193–210, 283–306, 386–98, 431–59; Khorasani, *Persian Archery and Swordsmanship*. 102–7; Smith, *Medieval Muslim Horsemanship*.

[30] This translation was in fact initially undertaken as a crucial preliminary step in approaching Monte's rather more challenging text. Monte's main sections relating to equestrianism are *Collectanea*, Book II chs. 66–103 (sig. d8r–e8r) and Book III colophon (sig. h1r); note also his material on throwing and vaulting referenced below, p. 39 fn. 75 and p. 41 fn. 78. A later, incomplete, and highly corrupt manuscript copy of Monte's original Spanish text survives in Madrid, Escorial Library a-IV-23. On Monte, see Anglo, "The man who taught Leonardo darts"; Fontaine, *Pietro del Monte*; Forgeng, "Pietro Monte's *Exercises*". Monte's nationality is the matter of some debate. Some scholars believe him to be Italian; while I believe he was born Pedro Monte, I here use the Italian version of his name to acknowledge the debate, while applying the name used of him during his professional career in Italy.

highly influential treatise in 1550.³¹ Aside from Duarte, Portuguese literature on the subject does not emerge until after 1600.³²

Duarte shares with other early equestrian writers an interest in the techniques and physical apparatus of riding: saddles, stirrups, spurs, bits and bridles, use of the hands and legs. His extensive exploration of physical principles—strength (*força*), steadiness (*assessego*), fluidity (*soltura*)—is more unusual among early works in the genre, though a familiar part of modern equestrian pedagogy, representing one aspect of the originality and insight that makes this work so unique among surviving writings of the Middle Ages: as Duarte himself tells us, the work is based not only on his personal experience, but on considered reflection on the subject matter (Prologue, III.7).³³

---

³¹ See Grisone, *Rules of Riding*; also Davis, *The Medieval Warhorse*, pp. 111–13; Deblaise, "Itinéraire du livre", pp. 254–59; Liedtke, *Royal Horse and Rider*, p. 89; Tomassini, *Italian Tradition*, pp. 79–102. For general background on the history of equestrian literature, see Cuneo, "Das Reiten"; Deblaise, *De Rusius à La Broue*; Felton, *Masters of Equitation*; *Glorious Horsemen*, pp. 40–46; Folger Shakespeare Library, *Reign of the Horse*; Grisone, *Rules of Riding*, pp. 25–29; Horst, *Great Books*; Huth, *Works on Horses and Equitation*; Liedtke, *Royal Horse and Rider*, pp. 89–90; Tomassini, *Italian Tradition*, pp. 49–60, 265–72; Wells, *Horsemanship*. This brief survey of equestrian literature does not include works dealing with the care and raising of horses, which has a much more substantial literary history extending back to antiquity.

³² For other early examples of equestrian literature from Portugal, see Andrade, *Arte de cavallaria*; Gallego, *Tratado da cavallaria*; Pacheco, *Tratado de cavallaria*; Peregra Rego, *Instruçaõ da Cavallaria*; see also Araújo, "Contributo para a história da alveitaria", p. 24; Bañuelos y de la Cerda, *Libro de la gineta*, pp. lxvi–lxxi; Huth, *Works on Equitation*, p. 28; Pereira, *Naissance et Renaissance*; Torrecilla, *Bibliografía Hípica*. Early Spanish writings on the subject are more plentiful: see Aguilar, *Tractado de la cavalleria*; Alcocer, *Tratado del juego*; Juan Arias de Avila, *Discurso para estar a la gineta*; Cespedes y Velasco, *Tratado de la Gineta*; Chacón, *Tractado de la cavalleria*, ed. Fallows; Fernandez de Andrada, *Naturaleza del cavallo*; Gali, *Las Reglas militares*; Manzanas, *Libro de enfrenamientos*; Navarrete, *Arte de enfrenar*; Suarez de Peralta, *Tractado de la cavalleria*; Puerto Carrero, *Discurso*; Vargas Machucha, *Libro de exercicios*; Villalobos, *Modo de pelear*.

³³ These important topics are similarly underplayed in early martial arts literature: almost entirely lacking from German writings on the topic, they appear in the Italian sources only briefly, notably in the allegorical *segni* of Fiore dei Liberi and Filippo Vadi (Malipiero, *Fior di battaglia*, fol. 34r; Vadi, *Arte Gladiatoria*, fol. 15r). Again, the closest parallels for Duarte are to be found in Monte, whose

Among the physical characteristics that Duarte discusses at length, *soltura* calls for some explanation. There is no precise modern English equivalent: it implies bodily relaxation, but also spontaneity and a mastery of technique that allows the physical exercise to be practiced in a flowing, easy fashion. Any modern practitioner of a physical art will recognize the importance of the concept, and the difficulty of reducing it to words. This translation renders the term as "fluidity" wherever possible, although in a few cases it resorts to "proficiency".[34]

Also unusual is Duarte's extensive treatment of psychological aspects of horsemanship such as fear and confidence (III.2 chs. 1–10, III.3 chs. 1–5, III.4 chs. 1–2, III.5 chs. 8–10), and of the moral analogies that can be derived from the practice (III.1 chs. 11, 19, 21). Attention to psychology is largely absent from early technical writings not only on horsemanship, but on any physical practice, including the martial arts, where psychology plays a critical role. Here again, striking parallels are to be found in Monte, who shows a comparable interest in psychology.[35]

Closely related to the psychology of horsemanship is Duarte's interest in the pedagogy of riding, another characteristic that distinguishes his work among technical treatises of the Middle Ages, which rarely deal explicitly with pedagogical issues. Duarte offers extensive advice on teaching novice riders, particularly children (II ch. 5); teaching how to wield the lance (III.4 ch. 5); teaching how to throw spears (III.4 ch. 13); and helping jousters overcome physical and psychological obstacles to success (III.4 ch. 6).[36]

Duarte's attention to the more abstract dimensions of his topic reflects his broader and deeper intellectual interests. While the work is full of discussions of physical principles, in particular strength and fluidity.

[34] The concept also figures prominently in Monte, in its adjectival forms: Sp. *disuelto* (cf. Madrid, Escorial Library a-IV-23, fol. 21v), It. *disciolto* (cf. *Collectanea*, sig. b5v) and Lat. *dissoltus* (cf. *Collectanea*, sig. f6v). Duarte's *soltura* intersects with Castiglione's *sprezzatura* (cf. Castiglione, *Courtier*, Bk. I ch. 26, p. 32), but is not quite the same thing.

[35] Monte, *De Dignoscendis Hominibus*, sig. &5v; Monte, *Collectanea*, Book I ch. 28 (sig. a5r), chs. 79–82 (sig. b8v), Book II ch. 1 (sig. c3v–c4r), ch. 80 (sig. e3r–v).

[36] Duarte's pedagogical interests are explored at length in Fernandes, "D. Duarte".

Livro do Cavalgar is a substantive technical treatise offering detailed and usable practical advice, the author positions his work within a broader literary and intellectual context than is typical of most writers on the subject. Duarte emphasizes the importance of literacy and familiarity with the literary heritage (III.5 ch. 15). Compared to *Leal Conselhero*, the *Livro do Cavalgar* makes few explicit references to literary sources, probably with an eye to keeping the work accessible to a non-scholarly readership. Nonetheless, Duarte does allude to the works of St. John Cassian, Giles of Rome, Vegetius, and Aristotle (III.5 chs. 1, 8–9, 14, 15), and the discussions of courage and great-heartedness are heavily indebted to Aristotle's *Nichomachean Ethics*, though probably at several removes (III.2 ch. 1, III.5 ch. 1).[37]

Medieval Horses and Equestrianism

Duarte's work is aimed at a readership of the mounted warrior-aristocracy—primarily male, though the connection of the manuscript to Queen Eleanor reminds us that women were also participants in medieval equestrian culture. The text is remarkably thorough and approachable as a technical treatise—aspiring modern riders might well find it a rewarding read—but it assumes a degree of prior technical knowledge of equestrianism that will be lacking in most readers today. The following pages offer a basic introduction to medieval equestrianism to assist in understanding Duarte's technical content.[38]

Medieval culture classified horses in several ways, notably function, breed, and color. Some horses were bred for warfare, including types known as the great horse, destrier, and courser; others were primarily for riding, such as the hackney (cf. III.2 ch. 5), palfrey, ambler, and pacer; and some served for labor, such as sumpters (packhorses) and carthorses. These categories were never absolute, since many

---

[37] On Duarte's textual sources, see Martins, *A Bíblia*, pp. 68–69.
[38] For some important introductory sources on medieval equestrianism and equestrian equipment, see Clark, *Medieval Horse*; Gelbhaar, *Reit- und Fahrzubehör*; Hyland, *Warhorse 1250–1600*; Tavard, *Sattel und Zaumzeug*. Important visual sources include Unterkircher, *King René's Book of Love*; Liedtke, *The Royal Horse and Rider*.

horses had to serve multiple purposes, and some types were specifically bred to serve more than one function—the rouncy was one example, usable either as a riding horse or as a light warhorse.

Breeds were most often categorized by their country of origin. Duarte mentions Sicilian horses (III.6 ch. 1), which were admired throughout Europe; other internationally important breeds included the Spanish, Lombard, and Arabian. Coloration has always been an easy way to identify individual horses, but medieval culture also took color as an indicator of a horse's personality and physical abilities. Duarte does not say much about the categories of horses, but he does reference various types, and he seems to have intended to focus more on the horse itself in sections 14 to 16 of Part III.[39]

Tack

Duarte begins his discussion of equestrian techniques and technology with several chapters on saddle-types and the styles of riding they require (III.1 chs. 1–6). The fundamental structure underlying the medieval saddle was the saddle-tree, consisting of four wooden components. A pair of panels or "bars" lay along the top of the horse's ribcage, parallel to the spine, serving to distribute the rider's weight onto the horse's ribs. These bars were secured to each other via connecting pieces that arched over the horse's spine in front and back. The front connector is often termed the pommel or saddlebow, the rear connector is the cantle. Padding underneath the tree protected the horse from chafing.

The tree apparatus was secured to the horse by a fabric or leather strap passing under the horse's belly, called the cinch or girth; some saddles were fitted with double girths, at the front and rear of the

---

[39] On horse classifications, see Ayton, *Knights and Warhorses*, 63–68; Gladitz, *Horsebreeding*, pp. 155–61. On internationally favored breeds, see Gladitz, *Horsebreeding*, pp. 162–65. A substantial portion of equestrian literature focuses on equine personalities and physiologies, often based on color and conformation. See Chacón, *Tractado de la Cavallería*, pp. xvi, 10–12; Gladitz, *Horsebreeding*, pp. 203, 238–39; Fallows, *Jousting*, pp. 296–97; Grisone, *Rules of Riding*, pp. 71–93.

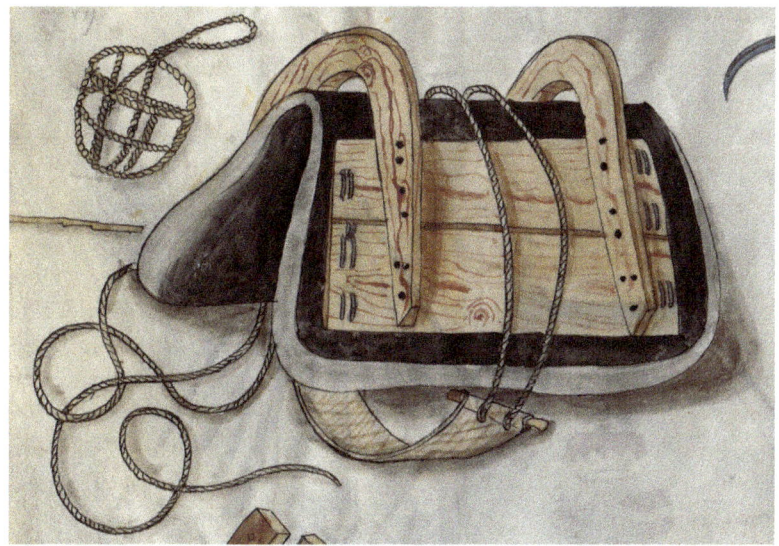

Plate 2. A pack-saddle, 1502 (Munich, Bayerische Staatsbibliothek Cod. icon. 222, fol. 23v). The image illustrates the basic structure of a saddle-tree: bars (with attached padding), pommel, cantle, and a girth, here designed to tie to itself rather than to the saddle (comparable to the modern surcingle).

saddle.[40] Surviving medieval saddles attached to the girth by a buckle and strap arrangement, as on a modern English saddle, but Duarte also mentions a strap called a latigo (II.1 ch. 17, III.7), which on modern Western saddles passes back and forth between rings on the saddle and girth, serving as a pulley system to tighten the girth. The simple pack-saddle mentioned by Duarte (*bardom*, III.1 ch. 6) consisted essentially of the components mentioned so far.[41]

More elaborate saddles added to this basic structure. Stirrups, hung from straps called stirrup-leathers, were suspended from the

---

[40] Cf. the double girth illustrated in Clark, *Medieval Horse*, half-title page, and Hickling, "Saddle of Henry V".

[41] Pereira, "Traité", (p. 149 n. 3) interprets the *bardom* as a training saddle (*bardelle*; Italian *bardella*, cf. Grisone, *Rules of Riding*, pp. 110–11) consisting of padded fabric and leather without a tree, but Duarte's use of the same word to describe a component of a normal riding saddle (III.1 ch. 17) makes "pack-saddle" or "saddle-tree" a more likely interpretation.

tree to add greater stability for the rider. For better comfort and appearance, the saddle could be covered with leather and/or fabric. A covered, and sometimes padded, seat made the tree more comfortable for the rider. Leather saddle-flaps provided a protective layer between the rider's thighs and the horse (*spendas*, III.1 ch. 16); the stirrup leathers might lie either over or under these flaps. Elaborate saddles might be further adorned with a decorative saddle-cover of cloth or leather (*funda*, III.1 ch. 16, III.7).[42]

War-saddles typically had an enlarged pommel and cantle, also termed the front and rear arçons (Port. *arçom*), providing additional protection and stability. The pommel structure might extend downwards to protect the rider's legs, with a concave shape to better accommodate them (cf. III.1 ch. 17); the top could extend upwards to cover the belly. The cantle might curve forward around the rider's hips to help stabilize him in combat. Since the cantle might absorb considerable impact, it was sometimes reinforced with iron struts that braced it against the bars of the saddle-tree (cf. III.1 ch. 9). Many saddles had padding inside the pommel and cantle to cushion the rider (cf. III.1 ch. 17, III.5 ch. 6).

The medieval war-saddle, with its high arçons, corresponds to the type that Duarte broadly labels "Brabant" saddles (*sellas de bravante*, cf. III.1 ch. 2). Duarte's French saddle, which he associates with non-specialized use, may be a low-cantled variant on this type (cf. III.6 ch. 2). The specific design of the saddle depended on its purpose: those for heavy cavalry tended to have higher pommels and cantles, those for lighter riding had lower ones.

The jousting saddle mentioned by Duarte (III.1 chs. 4, 14) is an extreme variant of the Brabant type, having a very deep pommel and cantle and a sharply angular seat shaped like an inverted V: the jouster stood in the stirrups, bracing against the cantle, rather than actually sitting on the saddle, which was not designed for comfortable riding. The rider might use extra cushions to help absorb the shock of impact (cf. III.5 ch. 6), and strapping could be applied to

---

[42] The meaning of Duarte's terms is difficult to verify from external sources, but their context here strongly supports this reading.

Plate 3. A horse with war saddle, c. 1460 (Biblioteca Apostolica Vaticana MS Ott. lat. 1417, fol. 22r). The saddle has a high pommel and cantle; the cantle curves around the hips, and is braced with iron struts.

the jouster's body to help stabilize him in the saddle (cf. III.1 ch. 14; III.5 chs. 5, 6).[43]

Toward the other end of the spectrum was the "jennet" saddle adopted from the Moors, having a relatively low pommel and cantle

---

[43] The cushions are alluded to by Monte, *Collectanea*, Book II ch. 101 (sig. e7r–v). Bindings for the body and stirrups are described (not very clearly) in Monte, *Collectanea*, Book II chs. 97–98 (sig. e6v–e7r) and ch. 101 (sig. e7r), mentioned in João I, *Montaria*, p. 26, and discussed in Gelbhaar, *Reit- und Fahrzubehör*, p. 81. Fallows, *Jousting*, pp. 131, 366, also mentions the practice, but here the allusion may simply be to the positioning of the stirrup within the forked band of the girth. The final illustration of the Getty manuscript of Fiore dei Liberi's early fifteenth-century *Flos Duellatorum* appears to show stirrups tied front and back to the double girths of the saddle (Los Angeles, J. Paul Getty Museum, MS Ludwig XV 13, fol. 47r, reproduced in Mondschein, *Knightly Art of Battle*, rear cover).

and a long seat, allowing it to be ridden with short stirrups and flexed legs.[44]

The typical European stirrup consisted of a loop of metal, flat across the bottom or "tread" where the rider's foot rested, and arching across the top, with a small loop at the apex to accommodate the stirrup-leather. The jennet saddle used trapezoidal-sided stirrups that encased most of the foot—Duarte calls them "covered stirrups" (*strebeiras cubertas*, III.1 ch. 16).[45] For some purposes, especially jousting, the stirrups might be secured in place with bindings (cf. III.1 chs. 4, 20).[46]

Bits and Bridles

One of the most important means of communication between the rider and horse is the contact between the rider's hand and the horse's mouth established through the reins (Port. *redeas*) and bit (Port. *freo*). The bit consists of a solid or jointed mouthpiece of metal that rests on the gummed "bars" of the horse's mouth, behind the front teeth and in front of the molars. The bit is held in the horse's mouth by the headstall (Port. *cabeçadas*), a system of leather straps around

---

[44] On the "Brabant" saddle, see Fallows, *Jousting in Medieval and Renaissance Iberia*, pp. 267–68. On brida and jennet saddles, see Bennett, *Conquerors*, pp. 115–21; Boeheim, *Waffenkunde*, p. 207; Machuca, *Gineta*, pp. 151–57; Puertocarrero, *Discurso*, pp. 18–20; Tavard, *Sattel und Zaumzeug*, 138–69; Tomassini, *Italian Tradition*, p. 132. On saddles in general, see Chacón, *Tractado de la Cavallería*, pp. 17–19; Demmin, *Kriegswaffen*, pp. 635–47; Demmin, *Arms and Armour*, pp. 355–60; Gelbhaar, *Reit- und Fahrzubehör*, pp. 170–84; Holme, *Academie of Armory*, 3.345, 396; Hyland, "The Medieval War Saddle"; Laking, *Record of European Armour and Arms*, 3.155–61, 170–76, 201–2; Monte, *Collectanea*, Book II chs. 88–91 (sig. e5r–e6r); Tavard, *Sattel und Zaumzeug*, 46–52, 74–82. An important surviving war saddle of Duarte's period is that of Henry V of England; see Hickling, "The Saddle of Henry V".

[45] On these stirrups, cf. also Boeheim, *Waffenkunde*, pp. 13–14; Fallows, *Jousting in Medieval and Renaissance Iberia*, pp. 281–82; Chacón, *Tractado de la Cavallería*, p. xli; Puertocarrero, *Discurso*, pp. 20–21; Zschille and Forrer, *Steigbügel*, pp. 16–18, pls. 17, 18. For a New World example, see Bennett, *Conquerors*, p. 122. On stirrups in general, see Demmin, *Kriegswaffen*, pp. 648–56; Demmin, *Arms and Armour*, pp. 361–65.

[46] On binding the stirrups, see also above, p. 21 fn. 43.

the horse's head. Collectively, the entire apparatus is known as the bridle (Port. *brida*).

Different horses have various levels of responsiveness to the bit: a horse who is relatively unresponsive is said to have a "hard mouth" (cf. III.5 ch. 5, III.5 ch. 13). Such horses called for a more severe bit, as did situations where extra responsiveness was required (cf. III.5 ch. 6). A wide variety of bit designs were developed to address the needs of various horses and uses, and there survives a substantial body of illustrated "bit-books" illustrating these designs, though the earliest date from the sixteenth century.[47] Duarte appears to have intended to go more deeply into the subject of bits in section III.13 of his work.

Most medieval European bits can be classed as snaffle or curb bits. The simplest and gentlest form was the snaffle, in which the reins attached directly to rings at the ends of the mouthpiece. More severe, and more typical for medieval warhorses, was the curb bit. Here the mouthpiece rotated on perpendicular "shanks" at its ends: the upper end of each shank fastened to a strap of the headstall passing behind the horse's head, and the lower end attached to the reins. When the reins were tensed, the leverage of the shank exerted a powerful action on the horse's mouth, while also exerting pressure on the back of the horse's head. This leverage was made possible by the curb (Port. *barbella*, III.5 ch. 7, III.6 ch. 2), a strap that fastened to the shanks of the bit, passing under the horse's chin. The curb acted as a fulcrum against the horse's jaw when the reins were tensed; it also made it harder for the horse to evade the pressure of the bit. The mouthpiece of the curb bit often arched upward inside the horse's mouth: when the reins were tensed, this arch or "port" pressed up against the horse's palate, further intensifying the pressure of the bit's action. The harsher action of the curb bit helped the rider control his horse amidst the stress and distraction of battle.[48] Some curb bits

[47] On bit-books, see Chénière, "Étude des mors aux XVIe et XVIIe siècles"; Cuneo, "Just a Bit of Control." Grisone includes an extensive section on bits in his *Rules of Riding* (pp. 269–93). Kreutzberger, *Warhaftige und Eygentliche Contrafactur*; Fouquet, *Traitté des embouchures*; Manzanas, *Libro de enfrenamientos*; Navarrete, *Arte de enfrenar*.

[48] On bits, see Boeheim, *Handbuch der Waffenkunde*, pp. 193–95; Clark, *Medieval Horse*, pp. 43–53; Demmin, *Kriegswaffen*, pp. 657–64; Demmin, *Arms and Armour*, pp. 366–68; Fallows, *Jousting in Medieval and Renaissance Iberia*,

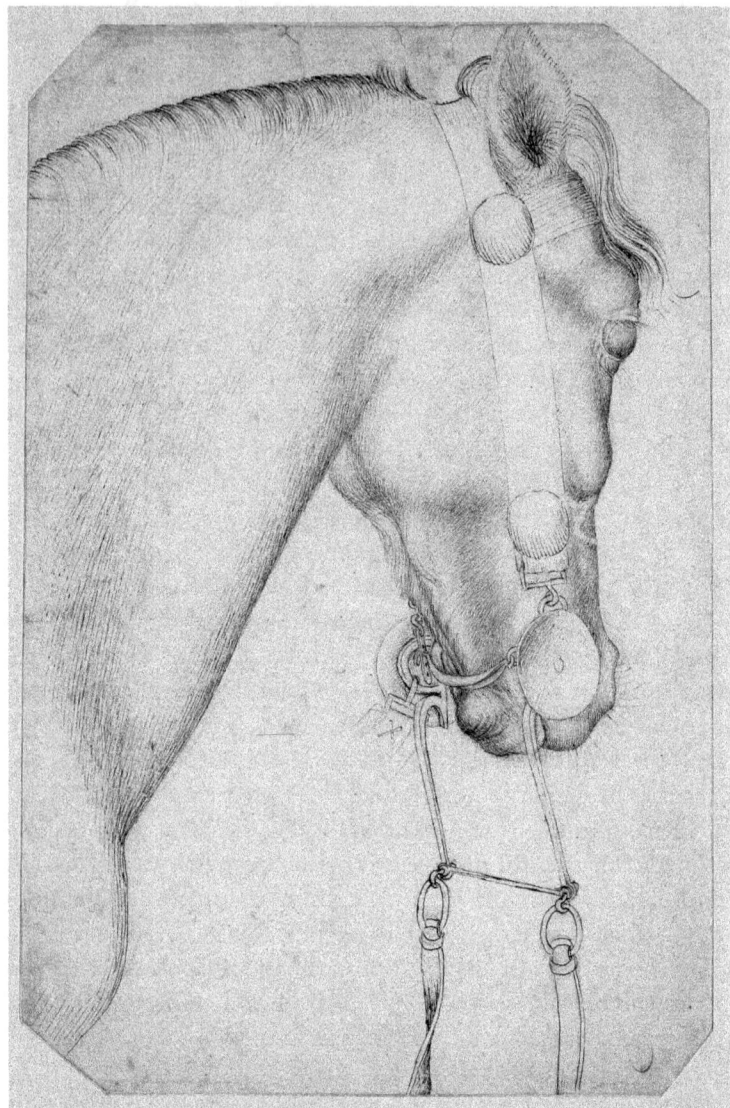

Plate 4. Sketch of a horse wearing a curb bit, by Antonio Pisanello, mid-1400s (Musée du Louvre, Inv. 2359, Recto, Fonds des dessins et miniatures). The curb can be seen passing under the horse's chin. A rein-ring, shaped like a reversed D, can be seen hidden behind the disk at the side of the mouth; attached to it is the hint of a rein-strap, indicating configuration as a double curb-snaffle bit.

were designed to accommodate two sets of reins, one attached to snaffle rings at the end of the mouthpiece, the other attached to the bottom of the shanks, allowing the bridle to function as either a snaffle or curb.

Duarte's scatch-bit (*brida d'escacha*, III.5 ch. 7) appears in sixteenth-century Italian texts as the *scaccia*, and in French as the *escache*. It is a variant of the curb bit having a jointed mouthpiece consisting of two cone-shaped rollers jointed apex to apex; the rollers have a textured surface and oval cross-section, a feature that softens the severity of the bit, as Duarte implies.[49] Duarte's *tari* bit remains a mystery (III.5 ch. 7): both Giese and Pereira suggest it may be a bit used with jennet gear, but the jousting context would be more consistent with some form of curb bit; a scribal error is also possible.[50]

The bit could be supplemented by an *enxacoma* (III.4 ch. 6), a form of noseband here translated by its cognate "hackamore", although it is unclear exactly what Duarte has in mind. Both the Arabic root *hakama* and the modern hackamore refer to nosebands. Duarte's *enxacoma* evidently helps steady or control the horse in jousting. Various versions of the noseband might serve to keep the horse's mouth closed, making it harder to evade the bit; or they could attach to a strap to keep the horse's head in the proper collected position, with the neck arched and nose downward; some versions even had serrations on the interior to increase the rider's control over the horse.[51]

---

pp. 268–70; Gelbhaar, *Reit- und Fahrzubehör*, pp. 9–36; Grancsay, *Equestrian Equipment*; Holme, *Academie of Armory*, 3.306; Hyland, *Warhorse*, pp. 7–9; Laking, *Record of European Armour and Arms*, 3.161–64; Markham, *Cavelarice*, 2.40–73; Tavard, *Sattel und Zaumzeug*, 65–69; Zschille and Forrer, *Pferdetrense*.

[49] On the scatch-bit, cf. Blundeville, *Horsemanshippe*, fols 57r–80r; Fallows, *Jousting in Medieval and Renaissance Iberia*, pp. 268–9, 376, 382 n. 52; Grisone, *Rules of Riding*, pp. 269, 421, 432, 433, 446–55, 457, 460, 556; Markham, *Cavelarice*, 2.50, 58–59; Pluvinel, *Maneige Royal*, p. 149 and fig. 51; Tomassini, *Italian Tradition*, p. 167.

[50] Giese, "Portugiesisches Reitzeug", p. 81; Pereira, "Traité," p. 145. For examples Zschille and Forrer, *Pferdetrense*, pl. XIII nos. 1–3, 5, pl XVIII nos. 3, 5, 6.

[51] On the *hakama* and hackamore, see Bennett, *Conquerors*, pp. 54–55, 123; Gelbhaar, *Reit- und Fahrzubehör*, p. 11; Hyland, *Medieval Warhorse*, pp. 94, 117; Ibn Hudhayl, *La parure des chevaliers*, transl. Mercier, p. 209.

Duarte's discussion of controlling the horse in jousting (III.5 ch. 7) also mentions cords that run from the girth or bridle to the rider's hands. Depending on configuration, these would serve to stabilize the rider, and possibly to keep the horse's head lowered. They can be compared to modern "draw reins" or "running reins", a pair of straps that run from the girth through the forelegs, to pass through rings on the bridle, and then to the rider's hand. A comparable apparatus is also mentioned in a fifteenth-century English list of equipment recommended for a joust of peace, helping the rider remain in the saddle: "a rein of Hungarian leather tied from the horse's head unto the girths between the forelegs of the horse against reversing".[52]

Spurs

Duarte discusses spurs briefly in III.1 ch. 18 and extensively in III.6 chs. 1–2. The medieval spur came in two basic types. The simple "prick" spur had a fixed spike at the heel, which might be more or less sharp depending on its use and the nature of the horse (cf. III.5 ch. 6). Jennet spurs were a variant of the prick type. The "rowel" spur had a rotating wheel of a multipointed star-shape.

Since the Brabant saddle required the rider to extend his legs, with his heels at some distance from the horse's flank, the accompanying spurs often had a long shaft to reach the horse. The elongated design appealed to the Gothic esthetic of late medieval Europe, and was often exaggerated in high-fashion spurs, a style Duarte disapproves. The stirrup-iron—the main metallic portion of the stirrup—was secured to the foot with leather straps, by means of buckles, hooks, or studs that hinged on rings at the terminal points of the iron.[53]

---

[52] Dillon, "MS Collection of Ordinances," p. 40.
[53] On spurs, see Clark, *Medieval Horse*, pp. 124–56; Demmin, *Kriegswaffen*, pp. 617–25; Demmin, *Arms and Armour*, pp. 342–49; Drugmand, "Eperonnerie"; Gelbhaar, *Reit- und Fahrzubehör*, pp. 91–116; Grancsay, *Equestrian Equipment*; Lacy, *History of the Spur*; Laking, *Record of European Armor and Arms*, 3.164–70; Zschille and Forrer, *Der Sporn*; Zschille and Forrer, *Reitersporen*.

Plate 5. Rowel spur, c. 1400. At the ends of the stirrup-iron are the pendant fittings that secured a leather strap under the heel. An additional leather passed over the instep.
Worcester Art Museum (MA), The John Woodman Higgins Collection, 2014.991. Image © Worcester Art Museum, All Rights Reserved.

Riding

As Duarte mentions, a horseman's manner of riding needed to be adapted to his equipment and circumstances: each style of equipment was optimized for riding in different ways for specific purposes. The classic riding style of the medieval knight is known by its Iberian name *brida* or "bridle" style, in which the rider's legs are extended and somewhat forward, the rider bracing toward the rear of the saddle, and often sitting against the cantle rather than in the seat. This position limited the degree of contact between the rider's legs and the horse, requiring a correspondingly heavier reliance on the bit for communication, typically using a curb bit. Brida riding was optimized for the armored heavy cavalry tactics of the medieval knight, and above all for the shock impact of attacking with a couched lance.[54]

Contrasting with the brida style was the Moorish-influenced jennet style (*gineta*, III.1 ch. 5), in which the rider sat in the center

---

[54] On brida riding, see Bachrach, "*Caballus* and *Caballarius*," p. 195; Bennett, *Conquerors*, pp. 99–100, 106–11, 140–41; Fallows, *Jousting in Medieval and Renaissance Iberia*, p. 267; Gelbhaar, *Reit- und Fahrzubehör*, pp. 79–81; Mercier, "Les écoles espagnoles"; Tavard, *Sattel und Zaumzeug*, 42–46, 52–53.

Plate 6. Christians and Moors in battle, from the *Altarpiece of St. George*, c. 1420s (Victoria and Albert Museum 1217–1864). The crowned figure in the center wields a couched lance, riding with his legs extended and forward in the brida style; the arçons of his saddle are relatively low, perhaps comparable to Duarte's "French" saddle; his horse is fitted with a double-reined bit incorporating both a snaffle and curb apparatus. His Moorish opponent carries a throwing spear and an *adarga* shield; he rides jennet-style, with his legs flexed; his stirrups are in the "covered" style typical for jennet riding.

of the saddle with his legs flexed and held closer to the horse's flanks. This type of riding allowed for more contact between the rider's legs and the horse, permitting closer communication between horse and rider, and facilitating the agile light-cavalry tactics favored by the Moors and eventually imitated by light cavalry in European armies.[55] The jennet style was particularly suited for spear throwing, since the rider could easily rise in the stirrups to put extra power and height behind the throw. Duarte also alludes to other styles of riding; his remark about Irish horsemen riding without stirrups (III.6 ch. 1) is corroborated in the twelfth century by Giraldus Cambrensis.[56]

While the shock tactics of heavy cavalry operations may have represented the core of chivalric horsemanship, this was not the limit of a knight's equestrian range: as Duarte points out, his readers might need to ride in different styles under various circumstances. The equestrian skills of the medieval knight were perhaps best showcased in the hunt, in which the unarmored aristocratic rider engaged in close-quarters confrontation with extremely dangerous prey: Duarte focuses on the bear and boar, and also mentions the bull—early versions of bullfighting were already in use.[57] As Duarte makes clear, equestrian hunting required extensive training for both horse and rider, and the stakes were high: incompetent riding could result in the death of horse or hunter. The skills involved were preserved into the modern age in the Iberian traditions of bullfighting, and Portugal today remains an important center of highly sophisticated equestrianism.

Duarte distinguishes four gaits: walk, trot, canter, and run (cf. III.5 ch. 4, III.5 ch. 5). The canter (*galopar*) and run (*correr*) call for

---

[55] On jennet riding, see Asín, "Origen Arabe", pp. 383–87; Bertrandon de la Broquière, *Voyage d'Outremer*, p. 220; Chacón, *Tractado de la Cavallería*; Fallows, *Jousting in Medieval and Renaissance Iberia*, pp. 272–84; Mercier, "Les écoles espagnoles"; Monte, *Collectanea*, Book III colophon (sig. h1r); Sanz Egaña, *Tres Libros de Jineta*, pp. viii–xli; Tapia y Salzedo, *Exercicios de Gineta*; Tavard, *Sattel und Zaumzeug*, 156–69. Cf. also Descoins, *Arab Equitation*.
[56] Cited Hyland, *Medieval Warhorse*, p. 103; Hyland, *Warhorse 1250–1600*, p. 7.
[57] On bullfighting during the period of Duarte, cf. Dionísio, "Recepção de D. Duarte", 368–69; Marques, *Portugal na Crise*, p. 483. See also Fallows, *Jousting*, pp. 284, 288–89; Machuca, *Gineta*, pp. 204–22. On hunting, see also Marques, *Portugal na Crise*, pp. 479–80.

some clarification for modern English-speaking readers. In modern English, gallop and canter refer respectively to the fast, four-beat gait (in which all four feet land at separate times), and to the slower three-beat gait (in which the horse's inside foreleg and outside hind-leg land simultaneously). The distinction does not appear until the eighteenth century, and most European languages continue to apply a cognate of "gallop" to both gaits. Duarte's "run" may be purely in reference to the horse's speed rather than to any distinction in the footfalls of the gait, though it would tend to correspond to the modern gallop.[58]

Lanceplay

One crucial piece of equestrian equipment in Duarte's treatise is the lance (discussed extensively in III.5 chs. 4–10): the horse, rider, and lance functioned as a single integrated system that can only be understood as a whole. Duarte uses the verb *reger* (here translated as "wield") with technical force to describe the use of the spear tucked under the armpit in the "couched" position. Duarte calls this position *so o braço*, "underarm", as opposed to using the weapon overhand as a spear, *sobremaão*. A rider using the spear underarm is said to "joust" (*justar*), even when hunting.

The lance of Duarte's period was about eleven feet long, usually made of ash. As Duarte mentions, it might be used with or without a lance-rest and grapper. The lance-rest (actually a lance-stop—the medieval English term was *arrest*) was a steel hook affixed to the right side of the breastplate, near the armpit. The grapper was a leather ring that slipped over the butt of the lance. When the lance was couched, the lance sat in the curve of the rest, with the grapper butting against the front of the rest. The rest served as a fulcrum to help manage the lance, and at the moment of encounter it transmitted the shock from the grapper into the wielder's breastplate and torso. By transmitting the impact directly to the core of the body, it reduced the risk of injury to the wielder's arm, while also reducing the play in the system, which allowed for a more powerful blow to the target.

---

[58] Grisone uses *correr* and *carriera* sometimes just as "run", but sometimes with technical force as "gallop" (*Rules of Riding*, pp. 200, 519).

Plate 7. A rider and horse equipped for jousting, 1460s (Vienna, Österreichische Nationalbibliothek, Codex Vindobonensis 2597, fol. 5v). The helmet is of the jousting type, strapped to the cuirass in the front and back as described by Duarte. The high pommel and cantle of the "Brabant" style of saddle is clearly visible, as is a notch to allow the butt of the lance to rest under the thigh. There is a triangular lance-rest at the right armpit, and a leather grapper on the lance just behind the jouster's hand. The rider wears prick spurs of moderate length.

Managing the lance in the couched position was challenging, and the weapon was normally carried upright or on the shoulder. When held upright, the butt might rest on the saddle or rider, with the lance angling forward and slightly to the right. As Duarte mentions, the butt could rest on the thigh; it could be wedged between the thigh and saddle; or it could be slipped into a small leather pouch attached to the rider's armor, saddle, or stirrup.[59] Getting the lance from the carrying position to the couched position was challenging, especially when the rider was armored, and Duarte offers careful instruction on how best to manage this: lifting the lance, clearing the armor, settling it into the rest, and finally lowering the point. The concluding action would be completed shortly before the "encounter" (*encontro*)—the universal term in Romance languages for the moment of impact with a couched lance.[60]

Duarte and the Horse

Duarte offers a tremendous amount of valuable detail about equestrian practices of the chivalric class: training, equipment, sports, even clothing. What is perhaps most striking is that he has very little to say about the animal. For all Duarte's interest in the psychology of the horseman, he largely ignores the psychology of the horse. This contrasts sharply with modern equestrianism, which encourages the rider to understand the horse's emotions in order to improve communication and control. An interest in horse psychology can be traced as far back as the treatises of the early modern period. In the

---

[59] Monte also mentions the pouch, but gives no details as to its configuration, aside from saying that it should be placed low with a heavy spear (*Collectanea*, Book II ch. 100, sig. e7r). On the pouch, see also Fallows, *Jousting*, pp. 98, 185–87, 214, 327, 391. The lance position is illustrated in Réné d'Anjou's 1457 manuscript of *Le Cueur d'Amours Espris* (Unterkircher, *King Réné's Book of Love*, fol. 5v).

[60] For other important sources on the handling of the lance, see Anglo, *Martial Arts*, pp. 227–70; Jean de Bueil, *Le Jouvencel*; Cruso, *Military Instructions*, pp. 36–37; Dall'Aggocchie, *Scrimia*, fols 58r–66r; Fallows, *Jousting*, pp. 187–91, 193–96; Gaier, *Technique*, pp. 7–10, 18–23; Markham, *Cavelarice*, pp. 245 ff.; Monte, *Collectanea*, Book II chs. 93–103 (sig. e6r–e8r); Pluvinel, *Maneige Royale*, pp. 109–40; Puertocarrero, *Discurso*, pp. 48–52; Juan Quijada de Reayo, *Doctrina del arte de la cavallería*, edited and translated in Fallows, *Jousting*, pp. 370–74; Luis Zapata de Chaves, "Del Justador", edited and translated in Fallows, *Jousting*, pp. 385–98. For important illustrations of the lance and its handling see Unterkircher, *King Réné's Book of Love*, fols 5v, 15r, 18v. Training for the lance is illustrated in the fourteenth-century *Roman d'Alexandre*, Oxford Bodleian MS 264, fols 82v, 100r; see also Monte, *Collectanea*, Book II ch. 100 (sig. e7r).

mid-1500s, Federico Grisone is clearly aware of the role of psychology in shaping a horse's relationship to the rider:

> Once the horse has experienced the beatings on the head and between the ears, it will be sufficient to punish him with a harsh voice, and with a very light touch which you can reduce or increase as his trickery reduces or increases, and even more when you know that he is naturally of two minds and of two hearts due to the quality of his coat and his markings. And know that there is no greater terror or punishment for him than the human voice. The voice will never confuse him, distract him, make him forget himself, humiliate him, make him flee, dishearten him, nor make him despair, as beatings with a stick will often do, although these often yield great results and from these arise infinite virtues as well. It is necessary that these should be used in a timely manner, followed by patting him. And with these methods, make him recognize that his own error was the cause of his punishment.[61]

A century later William Cavendish, duke of Newcastle, backhandedly acknowledges that the horse is a thinking, feeling creature whose internal world parallels that of human beings, emphasizing that the horse's emotions play a major rôle in the equestrian equation:

> No man in the world, no, not the wisest, if he were put into the form of a horse ... could find more subtle ways to oppose a man than a horse will; nay, nor near so many, I dare say. Whence I conclude that the horse must know you are his master: that is, he must fear you, then he will love you for his own sake. Fear is the sure hold, for fear doth all things in this world, love little, and therefore let your horse fear you.[62]

Such reflections on equine psychology are conspicuously lacking in Duarte's work. In part this may reflect the incomplete state of the text: the unwritten sections 14 to 16 of Part III are precisely those which might have had the most to tell us about Duarte's understanding of horse psychology. Yet the very fact that Duarte chose to

---

[61] Grisone, *Rules of Riding*, p. 342–43.
[62] Cavendish, *New Method*, pp. 200–1. On Newcastle's engagement with the psychology of horses, see Walker, "Author of their Skill".

prioritize his chapters on human fear and confidence over any discussion of equine emotion itself reflects the author's anthropocentric orientation.

Duarte's lack of interest in the horse's mentality may warn us against sentimentalizing the relationship between these animals and their chivalric riders. Duarte's work suggests that the medieval knight may not have had a deep connection to the animal he rode: like many traditional equestrian cultures around the world, knights may have looked at their horses as expendable commodities—not to be carelessly wasted, but not something in which they were emotionally invested. Such an interpretation may be suggested by Duarte's language: he normally does not refer to the "horse" (*cavalho*) but the "animal" (*besta*, here rendered "mount" as a less cumbersome translation); it is also supported by the passage in III.1 ch.15 where Duarte rates embarrassment of the rider as a more serious concern than the death of his horse.[63]

The *Livro do Cavalgar* and Other Technical Domains

Duarte's equestrian subject matter intersects with other topics and genres. A considerable portion of the work relates to hunting (III.4 chs. 11–13), a subject for which there is a significant body of medieval writings, going back as far as the thirteenth-century *La chace dou cerf*, and including the *Livro da Montaria* by Duarte's father.[64] Another well developed medieval genre that intersects with the *Livro do Cavalgar* is the literature of veterinary medicine, as Duarte himself mentions (II ch. 2, III Introduction).[65]

---

[63] By way of comparison, one might look at reactions to horse injuries in settings like the joust, as documented in sources such as the Passo Honroso (Fallows, *Jousting*, pp. 451, 488, 491).

[64] See Cummins, *Hound and the Hawk*; Hobusch, *Fair Game*; Phoebus, *The Hunting Book*. On hunting in medieval and early modern Portugal, see Andrade, *Cavalleria*, pp. 292–336; João I, *Monteria*; Monteiro, *A Guerra em Portugal*, pp. 416–19; and the bibliography in Torrecilla, *Bibliografía Hípica*.

[65] On medieval Portuguese veterinary literature, see Araújo, "Contributo para a história da alveitaria", pp. 22–23; Dias, *Arte de ser Bom Cavaleiro*, pp. 19–21; Gomes, *Court Society*, pp. 194–95; Pereira, "Le Cheval"; Vasconcelos, "Livro

The *Livro do Cavalgar* also stands as an important milestone in the history of writing about sports and physical culture.[66] Aside from hunting and martial arts, sports literature from the Middle Ages is quite rare. Even jousting and tourneying are not extensively covered in technical writings of the period. Technical details about tournament sports are offered in a few texts such as the fourteenth-century Castilian regulations of the Order of the Band, the fifteenth-century *Traictié de la forme et devis d'ung tournoy* by Réné d'Anjou, and Ponç de Menaguerra's *Lo Cavaller*, published in 1493; but the primary focus is always on the logistics of organization or the rules of the sport, with very little detail about the physical techniques of the participants.[67] Aside from Duarte, the only extensive discussion of the techniques of tournament combat that could possibly be classed as medieval is in Pietro Monte.[68] Only after 1500 does one find a body of comparably detailed writings on the subject.[69]

---

dalveitaria"; Vasconcelos, "Mestre Giraldo"; and the bibliographical guide by Palau Claveras, *Bibliografía hispánica de veterinaria y equitación anterior a 1901*, pp. 1–4. On medieval veterinary literature in general, see also Davis, *Medieval Warhorse*, pp. 100–7.

[66] On early sports literature, see Cram, Forgeng, and Johnston, *Francis Willughby's Book of Games*, pp. 43–47; McClelland, *Body and Mind*, pp. 19–59.

[67] See Anglo, "Jousting—the earliest treatises", p. 10; Fallows, *Jousting*, pp. 323–62; Réné d'Anjou, *Traité de la forme et devis d'un tournoi*. On tournament literature, see Anglo, "How to Win at Tournaments", pp. 252–55; Barber and Barker, *Tournaments*, pp. 67–69. For the Order of the Band, see Ceballos-Escalera y Gila, *Banda Real*; Fallows, *Jousting*, p. 1. The text was copied into Alonso de Cartagena's *Doctrinal de los Caballeros*, edited in Fallows, *Tratados Militares*, pp. 311–12. For an edition and translation of Menaguerra, see Fallows, *Jousting*, pp. 323–62.

[68] Monte, *Collectanea*, Book II chs. 93–103 (sig. e6r–e8r); for a much briefer discussion of the topic, see Jean de Bueil, *Le Jouvencel*, II.100–2. On jousting literature, see Anglo, "Jousting—the earliest treatises"; Anglo, "How to Win at Tournaments", pp. 255–61; Anglo, *Martial Arts*, pp. 227–38; Fallows, *Jousting in Medieval and Renaissance Iberia*. For later Portuguese material on the subject, see Andrade, *Arte de cavallaria*, pp. 223–46, 504–28.

[69] Anglo, *Martial Arts*, pp. 238–47; Fallows, *Jousting in Medieval and Renaissance Iberia*, p. 1. See above on lanceplay for additional sources on jousting.

Duarte discusses both of the main forms of tournament sports of the period, the tourney and the joust.[70] The tourney, sometimes termed a mêlée, involved two teams of riders striking at each other with blunt cudgels or swords—in some cases the goal was to strike off the heraldic crests fastened to the rider's helms, but usually the outcome was determined by a qualitative evaluation of their performances by a panel of judges, as implied by Duarte's advice that the tourneyer should choose tactics that maximized his visibility and impressiveness (III.5 ch. 14).

The joust pitted individual riders against each other, charging one another with lances. Jousts could take a variety of forms: the version described by Duarte is a variant of the "joust of peace", involving specialized equipment designed specifically for the sport, in contrast with the "joust of war", which used battlefield equipment with only a few modifications for added safety. In the joust of peace, the jousters wore armor that was more encumbering and protective than battlefield armor, including a jousting helm strapped to the torso armor in front and back for greater rigidity (III.5 ch. 6). This helm maximized protection to the jouster at the cost of mobility and vision, though contrary to the persistent myth, the jouster did not lean back at the moment of impact to close off his eyeslot against shards from a shattered lance—a myth clearly debunked by Duarte's emphasis on the importance of keeping one's eye on the target (III.5 ch. 6).[71]

The lance had a three-pronged "coronel" point that spread the impact, increased the likelihood of a dramatic hit, and prevented penetration of the eyeslot. Such lances also had a conical steel vamplate that slipped over the shaft just in front of the hand, providing extra protection to the wielder. Duarte refers to the jousting lance as a *vara*, the usual Iberian term for the lance used in the joust of peace; *lança* is his generic term for any form of spear.[72]

---

[70] On tournament sports in general, see Barber and Barker, *Tournaments*; Clephan, *Tournament*; Fallows, *Jousting*, pp. 1–9; Nickel, "Tournament". On tournament sports in medieval Portugal, see Marques, *Portugal na Crise*, p. 481; Marques, *Sociedade*, pp. 202–5; Monteiro, *A Guerra em Portugal*, pp. 419–32. On Duarte's own participation in jousting, see Zurara, *Crónica*, p. 73.

[71] Monte makes the same point about keeping the eyes open (*Collectanea*, Book II ch. 96, sig. e6v).

[72] Cf. Riquer, "Las armas en el *Victorial*", p. 248–49.

The *Livro do Cavalgar* and Other Technical Domains 37

Plate 8. A joust of peace, 1480s (British Library, MS Cotton Julius E IV, fol. 15v). The lances are fitted with three-pronged coronel points and vamplates to protect the hand, and the jousters wear tilting-shields that serve as targets for the opponent. Between them is a wooden tilt, and in the center a liveried attendant holds a pair of jousting saddles.

Jousters often wore shields that served as a target for their opponent, although hits on the helm were considered superior to those on the shield (cf. III.5 ch. 10). Duarte's jousters are separated from each other by a barrier called a tilt (*tea*), a relatively recent invention that appears to have originated in Iberia. Originally made of cloth on a wooden framework, during the fifteenth century a fully wooden tilt became the norm.⁷³

Plate 9. Lance-tip of coronel form, early 1500s.
Worcester Art Museum (MA),
The John Woodman Higgins Collection, 2014.668.
Image © Worcester Art Museum, All Rights Reserved.

---

[73] On the tilt, see Barber and Barker, *Tournaments*, pp. 194–96; Clephan, *Tournament*, pp. 39, 67; Fallows, *Jousting*, pp. 92–94.

Duarte also mentions the distinctively Iberian tournament sport of *jogo de canhas*, "cane games" (III.5 ch. 10). This sport had Moorish origins, and derived from the tactics of Moorish cavalry: the opposing teams would take turns hurling light javelins made of reeds, the defending team protecting themselves with the *adarga*, a leather shield used by Moorish cavalry and adopted by Christian Iberians as well.[74]

Apart from cane games, throwing sports were well established as a chivalric pastime, serving to hone battlefield and hunting skills as well as fostering physical strength and agility. Duarte offers considerable technical detail on throwing, with specific recommendations on how to throw spears both on foot and on horseback (III.4 ch. 13). Duarte's discussion of throwing is again paralleled in Monte's writings.[75] Duarte's reference to a sport called *dardo*, here translated "javelin" (III.5 ch. 13), remains obscure. The modern game of darts does not appear to have been known in the Middle Ages, though not all games are well documented. Duarte is probably referring to a much larger, though still light, spear-like projectile. "Javelin" may be the closest modern equivalent, though the context suggests that the game was played for accuracy rather than distance.

Duarte also makes reference to vaulting on horseback as practiced both by the ancient Romans and by his contemporaries (III.4 ch. 14). This martial sport is attested as early as the fifth-century military treatise by Vegetius; the passage was referenced by the ninth-century

---

[74] On the *jogo de canhas* and its Spanish equivalent, the *juego de cañas*, see Andrade, *Arte de cavallaria*, pp. 188–222; Andrade, *Luz*, pp. 411–16, 420–23; Barber and Barker, *Tournaments*, pp. 163–64; Chacón, *Tractado de la cavallería*, ed. Fallows, pp. xxv, 35–38; Fallows, *Jousting in Medieval and Renaissance Iberia*, pp. 284–94; Fuchs, *Exotic Nation*, pp. 89–102; Harris, *Aztecs, Moors, and Christians*, pp. 54–63; Machuca, *Gineta*, pp. 223–37; Puertocarrero, *Discurso*, pp. 58–59; Tapia y Salzedo, *Gineta*, pp. 79–93; Tomassini, *Italian Tradition*, pp. 26–27. A comparable sport is documented in more recent times among North African Arabs; Mercier calls it *jerid* (Ibn Hudhayl, *La parure des chevaliers*, transl. Mercier, pp. 401–2).

[75] Monte, *De Dignoscendis Hominibus*, sig. z3r–z8v; Monte, *Collectanea*, Book I chs. 19–23 (sig. a4v), Book II chs. 129–140 (sig. f3v–f4v). See also Cram, Forgeng, and Johnston, *Francis Willughby's Book of Games*, pp. 160, 258; João I, *Montaria*, pp. 13, 295, 426–28; Giles of Rome, *De Regimine Principum* III.7, 15; Puertocarrero, *Discurso*, pp. 48–49.

Plate 10. "Stirrups", plate 9 from the series *Nova Reperta* (New Discoveries), Theodor Galle, about 1570–1633, after Johannes Stradanus (Flemish, 1523–1605), about 1580. At left a rider tests his stirrups for throwing.
Worcester Art Museum (MA), 2006.9
Image © Worcester Art Museum, All Rights Reserved.

Frankish Benedictine Rabanus Maurus, who noted that the Franks also practiced vaulting.[76] The sport is mentioned in Duarte's day in the biography of Boucicault: according to his biographer, the renowned knight would "leap from the ground onto a large man mounted on a large horse to ride on his shoulders, only grabbing him by the sleeve to help himself up; and placing one hand on the pommel of the saddle on a large horse, with the other grabbing the mane near its ears, he would spring over his arms from the ground to the other side of the horse".[77] Boucicault's feats seem astonishing, even improbable, to the modern reader, but Pietro Monte in the late 1400s describes an extensive repertoire of comparably demanding equestrian stunts, each with its own evocative name—the *galeazzia*, the *montesina*, the *maura*, the *schiavonesca*. By this time, the mar-

[76] Davis, *Warhorse*, p. 14.
[77] Lalande, *Jehan le Maingre*, pp. 25–26.

tial origins of vaulting can be hard to detect underneath the courtly athlete's exhibitionism, although Monte like Duarte emphasizes its value in fostering strength and agility.[78]

In addition to his advice on using the lance, Duarte offers some technical specifics for the use of the sword on horseback (III.5 ch. 14); both topics intersect with the literature of martial arts, a subject that has left a significant body of medieval writings, although Duarte remains one of the earliest known authors.[79] In fact, this is not Duarte's only text on the subject: in the compendium known as the *Livro da Cartuxa* he also left a short memorandum on a routine for training in arms:

> **Regimen for learning some things in arms**
> On certain days at the hour of tierce we do training, and the training is as follows. The trainee gets fully armed and runs up a slope for a goodly distance as hard as he can. Then he returns home, and there we have good iron armor for visitors to use, and also spears, axes, and swords of wood; and when the trainee wants to spar with someone, he gets equipped with arms half again as heavy as those he would actually use on the day of battle. The sparring that he does with these people allows him to learn techniques, defences, and attacks that others know. And if nobody comes for eight or ten days to train with him, he can train with whomever he will. This practice allows him

---

[78] Monte, *De Dignoscendis Hominibus*, sig. y8v–z2v; Monte, *Collectanea*, Book I chs. 26–27 (sig. a5r), Book II chs. 141–146 (sig. f4v–f6v). On vaulting in the Middle Ages and the Renaissance, see Andrade, *Arte de cavallaria*, pp. 340–55; Bascetta, *Sport e Giuochi*, 1.49–106; Cram, Forgeng and Johnston, *Book of Games*, p. 271; Delcampe, *L'art de monter à cheval*; Fontaine, "La voltige à cheval"; Fouquet, *Traitté des embouchures*; Imbotti de Beaumont, *L'escuier françois*; McClelland, *Body and Mind*, pp. 55, 77; Schmidt, "Trois dialogues de l'exercise de sauter et voltiger en l'air: Strategies of Ennoblement of a Bodily Practice in the Sixteenth Century"; Stokes, *The Vaulting Master*; Wallhausen, *Ritterkunst*, pp. 72–76.

[79] Anglo, *Martial Arts of Renaissance Europe*, pp. 22–27. On early martial arts treatises from Portugal and Spain, see Leguina, *Libros de Esgrima*; Leguina, *Bibliografia e Historia*; Sousa Viterbo, *Esgrima*. On early texts from Germany, see Forgeng and Kiermayer, "The Chivalric Art"; Forgeng, "Owning the Art". For early Italian sources, see Mondschein, *Knightly Art of Battle*; Vadi, *Gladiatoria*; see also Forgeng, "Pietro Monte's *Exercises*".

to develop good breath, and to learn from various people in feats of arms.[80]

Duarte's remarks on swordplay in the *Livro do Cavalgar* connect to the mainstream of medieval writings on the subject, though other texts mostly deal with combat on foot. His terms for the main attacks match those in other Romance treatises: *talho* (forehand cut), *revés* (backhand cut), *fendente* (vertical downward cut), and *ponta* (thrust). His reference to the diagonal downward blow as the most powerful recalls the content of contemporary German treatises, which call this the *Zornhaw*, "wrath cut".[81]

The *Livro do Cavalgar* also discusses wrestling, an activity with important martial applications in the close-quarters combat of the armored knight. In one passage Duarte discusses the techniques of wrestling on horseback (III.1 ch. 20), in the other he addresses wrestling on foot (III.5 ch. 16). The former mentions both sporting and earnest contexts; the latter leans toward wrestling as a sport, though both Duarte and other writers see the sport as providing valuable physical and mental conditioning for the warrior.[82]

As Duarte himself acknowledges, wrestling on foot seems out of place in a treatise on horsemanship. Duarte is so worried about the mismatch that he admonishes future scribes not to skip this material in copying his book (III.5 ch. 16). He does somewhat justify this chapter on the grounds that wrestling contributes to a rider's general *soltura*. But the insertion of this material near the end of the pre-1433 portion of the book suggests that the author simply wanted to get it into writing while he had the chance: capturing the information, a priority Duarte mentions in his Prologue, may have taken on new importance as the aging prince saw looming before him the prospect of full monarchical responsibilities. Both the internal evidence of the

---

[80] Duarte, *Livro dos Conselhos*, p. 270.
[81] Cf. Monte, *Collectanea*, Book I ch. 11 (sig. a3r); Forgeng, *Lecküchner*, pp. 438, 443.
[82] Cf. Monte, *De Dignoscendis Hominibus*, sig. x3r–y6r; Monte, *Collectanea*, Book I chs. 3–10 (sig. a2r–a3r), Book II chs. 2–8 (sig. c4r–c7v). Monte, *Collectanea*, Book II ch. 79 (e3r) discusses wrestling on horseback. For other medieval sources on wrestling, see Anglo, *Martial Arts*, pp. 172–86; Forgeng and Kiermayer, "Chivalric Art", pp. 160–61.

text and the biographical sketch by Rui de Pina suggest that Duarte had a particular fondness for the sport.

Somewhat surprising is the relative paucity of reference to specifically martial applications of equestrian skills. Duarte justifies his work based on the usefulness of horsemanship to soldiers, and the skills of equestrian wrestling, throwing, and close combat with lance and sword have obvious relevance to warfare. Yet aside from a very brief reference to the kinds of sword-blows most useful against mounted or pedestrian opponents, there are few specific references to military applications of Duarte's techniques.[83] Half a century later, Pietro Monte would express misgivings about sharing martial secrets with unknown readers who might put them to evil use; perhaps similar reservations have informed Duarte's reticence on specifically military uses of the equestrian arts.[84]

---

[83] For specifically military applications, see II.5 ch. 12, II.5 ch. 14. On mounted combat, see Anglo, "How to Win at Tournaments", pp. 253–55; Anglo, *Martial Arts*, pp. 253–70; Monte, *Collectanea*, Book II chs. 66–103 (sig. d8r–e8r).

[84] Monte, *De Dignoscendis Hominibus*, sig. &2r.

Note on the Translation

Duarte's prose is generally easy to follow, and this translation attempts to capture the matter-of-fact style of the original, although both the original and the translation become more dense where Duarte reflects on the philosophical implications of his subject—Duarte is often faulted by modern Portuguese readers for the Latinity of his vocabulary and syntax, which is certainly true of these passages, though less so of others.[85] The greatest challenges to interpretation arise where the author's technical subject matter takes us into topics that were accessible to his readers but are not fully recoverable from the evidence that survives half a millennium later. This is especially true of the section on wrestling, where Duarte himself acknowledges that the text will be incomprehensible to those who are not already familiar with the topic, and advises readers to seek explanation from an expert. In such cases, the footnotes provide such information as is available, but otherwise the translation respects the opacity of the original. Similarly, some of the technical sections, such as those on wielding the lance or chasing down quarry from horseback, deal with complex physical situations that do not lend themselves easily to verbal expression. In most cases, sustained close reading and reflection will allow a reader to untangle these passages, but some ambiguities remain, and the translation tries to avoid imposing an artificial and deceptive clarity.

The translation is based on Piel's edition of 1944, accepting his readings unless otherwise noted. Alterations or insertions relative to the manuscript original are flagged with square brackets.

Portions of the text were previously translated into English by Amélie Hutchinson in Richard Barber and Juliet Barker, *Tournaments*, pp. 197–205 and by Sydney Anglo in "Jousting – the earliest

---

[85] On Duarte's language, see Marques, *Leal Conselheiro*, pp. 21–22; Maués, "As ensinanças do livro do cavalgar", pp. 211, 213, 228–32.

treatises", pp. 5–9. The entire text has been translated into English as *The Royal Book of Jousting, Horsemanship, and Knightly Combat* by Antonio Franco Preto and Luís Preto (2005), but this translation is full of errors and cannot be relied on.

References to the text are by Part, Section, and Chapter numbers: "III.3 ch. 5" refers to Part III, Section 3, Chapter 5.

The Book of Horsemanship
by Duarte I of Portugal

[Prologue]

In the name of our Lord Jesus Christ, with His grace and that of the Virgin Mary, His very holy mother, our Lady: here begins the book of instruction for riding well in every type of saddle, composed by King Dom Eduarte, king of Portugal and the Algarve and lord of Ceuta, who started this book when he was still a prince.

In the name of our Lord Jesus Christ: It is ordained that we should be accomplished in all things, and as the saying has it, "Of making books there is no end";[1] and so for my own diversion and enjoyment, and recognizing that the art of being a good horseman is one of the most important skills that lords, knights, and squires ought to possess, I am writing a few things to assist the development of those who read this book with good will and are willing to do as I instruct.

You should know first of all that you will attain this art more by native talent, by acquiring and maintaining good mounts and having the opportunity to ride them regularly, and by living in a household and country that breeds and values good horsemen, than by knowing anything I will write here, or could be written by those who know more about it than I do, in the absence of good and continuous practice and the other advantages I have just listed. But I am writing

---

[1] The saying can be traced to Ecclesiastes 12:12. However, Duarte's immediate influence may be Alonso de Cartagena, who uses it in the invocations of his early works, such as *Memoriale virtutum* (commissioned by Duarte circa 1422) and his translation into Castilian of Cicero's *De officiis* (1422), to support the rhetorical trope of *ars longa, vita brevis*. Cartagena composed both of these works during his diplomatic missions to Portugal, and they were almost certainly familiar to Duarte. See Cartagena, *Memorial de virtudes*, ed. Campos Souto, p. 202, and Cartagena, *Libros de Tulio: De senetute; De los ofiçios*, ed. Morrás, p. 206 (and p. 389, nn. 34 and 37); also Dionísio, 'Do Memoriale Virtutum, de Alfonso de Cartagena, ao Leal Conselheiro, de D. Duarte', pp. 274–75.

this book to teach those who do not know about such things, and for those who know more, to consolidate in the memory those things that seem good to them, and so that they can teach others, correcting the errors I discuss.

Those who wish to possess this art need to have the three main things through which one acquires any art:

> Great will,
> adequate ability,
> and much knowledge.[2]

I will express my opinions concerning each of these; and even though ability and will cannot really be taught—since in all matters they are granted by nature and special grace rather than by learning—I will write about them to whet the desire and show the ability that we all possess, if we have the will and knowledge.

Some people would say that I should not devote so much effort to writing such a treatise, given that I always have other pressing matters to deal with; and also considering that everyone learns this art by himself, so there is no point writing about it. Here is my response—by way of excuse, and to offer others who wish to create such works an example through my own approach.

I have read that the heart of man is like a mill: driven by the force of the waters, it never ceases its motion, and it produces whatever flour comes from the seed it grinds.[3] We make our heart work on whatever we allow it to think about most: if it is not given good things to keep it busy, since it needs to focus on something, it will soon turn to vices, which are the root of all wickedness, unless we periodically provide other material, to keep it occupied with something besides evil thoughts when it has space and leisure.

The valiant emperor Julius Caesar was of this opinion, so to keep himself busy, no matter how much he had to do, whenever he had

---

[2] These three topics define the three main parts of the book.
[3] Duarte is alluding to Saint John Cassian (c. 360–435), *Collationes patrum Sceticorum*, composed some time after 420 (col. 507). This work is available in English translation: see Cassian, *The Conferences*, trans. Ramsey, *First Conference (The First Conference of Abba Moses: On the Goal and End of the Monk)*, Chapter XVIII.1, p. 57. pdf 269

a free moment he pursued studies and wrote new books.[4] My own heart cannot always attend to what might be best and most useful for someone of my position in society. Some days my mind was at leisure even though my body was working—when I was out hunting, hawking,[5] and traveling, or when court officials were late for meetings. At such times, to keep my mind from matters that might lead to trouble, and to draw other people away from things I disapproved of, I found it a good and beneficial remedy to think and to write by my own hand about this topic, owing to the fascination and pleasure I derive from it; otherwise I would never do it, for I fully recognize what good it does or does not do me.

To those who say that this art cannot be learned from a book, I grant that this is true. But I think most people will greatly benefit from reading carefully what I write. And because I know of no-one else who has really written about it, it pleases me to be the first to put this science into writing, and to intersperse some things relating to our customs, even though they may not be wholly pertinent to the subject, because they may benefit some readers, even if others find them superfluous.

I recognize that for a nobleman to have knowledge in only a single art cannot be greatly advantageous, yet diffuse power is certainly weaker than if it is consolidated.[6] Still, by interacting with many people of various estates and areas of knowledge, it stands to reason that we can acquire knowledge of more things than other people, as long as we possess natural understanding. Therefore my will urges

---

[4] The immediate source for this comment is Cicero's *De Officiis*, III.1. Duarte had access to a Castilian translation of this work composed in 1421–22 by Alonso de Cartagena while he was in residence at Duarte's court, and a Portuguese translation composed shortly after 1433 by the Infante Pedro, Duke of Coimbra and dedicated to Duarte. Both translations are now available in modern critical editions. See Cartagena, *Libros de Tulio*, ed. Morrás, p. 316, and *Livro dos oficios de Marco Tullio Ciceram*, ed. Piel, p. 149.

[5] Hawking: *Caça* normally means hunting small game, as opposed to *montaria* (here translated as "hunting"), the pursuit of large game, especially boars. But Duarte appears to use *caça* to refer specifically to hawking; cf. below, p. 135 fn. 27.

[6] Duarte here echoes a phrase used by his father: *a virtude ajuntada he mais forte que as que som espargidas* (João I, *Livro da Montaria*, p. 15); cf. also Monte, *Collectanea*, Book I ch. 70 (sig. b6r).

me to write about things I have heard or arrived at through reason, believing that people can derive good advice from them without any disadvantage.

Anyone who wants to absorb this well should read this book from the beginning, bit by bit, slowly, and taking careful note of everything, sometimes returning to what they have already read in order to understand it better. For if they read it straight through without interruption, as if it were a book of stories, it will soon frustrate them and make them impatient, because they cannot fully understand or remember it; for it is a general rule that this is how we should read any book of science or instruction.[7]

Here begins Part I of this book, which deals with the Will

Chapter 1: Reasons why knights and squires should be good horsemen, given the benefit and honor that comes from this skill

Since all men naturally desire honor, profit, and proper pleasure, it seems to me that all lords, knights, and squires should greatly desire this art, seeing how it engenders these benefits for those who practice it well. As to honor and profit, it would take a long time to recount how in the wars of the king, my lord and father (may God have his soul) and in other wars, many men have acquired great fame, estates, and benefits with considerable help from this art. This stands to reason, for good horses are one of the greatest advantages for men who go to war. One can well understand the great advantage that good horsemen have in actions of war over those who are lacking in this art, presuming they are adequately endowed with other pertinent qualities, even if they do not excel in them. Horsemanship is one of the best skills for warriors to possess, and in great deeds people profit very little from good horses if they do not know how to ride well in the manner required by the action in which they have to use them. For some riders are good horsemen in one kind of saddle, but not in others. Likewise some, being seen on horseback in civilian

---

[7] Duarte gives much the same advice in the prologue to *Leal Conseilheiro* (p. 10).

clothes simply running their horses, would be thought to know little about riding in the opinion of those who know it well, while being armed for the joust, they could not truly be faulted. And so it is with everything you have to do on horseback: some have great advantage over others, depending on how they are naturally inclined and whether they have the opportunity for extensive practice and good instruction.

But a knight or squire who knows little about horsemanship deserves to be judged by knowledgeable people as someone who lacks one of the most beneficial arts for those who know it properly. For aside from other advantages, it greatly nourishes courage. I have verified this by what I have seen of youths and other men of weaker disposition: they will freely admit that on foot they do not feel capable of doing what good and valiant men do, but on horseback, if they are knowledgeable about this art and have a good will, they quickly realize that they have the advantage over others—even those who have good wills—if they know that the others are lacking in this art. And indeed they feel this advantage in many other things required in war. Also it inspires them to breed good horses, because they realize how helpful they are, and to know and maintain them well, and to cultivate their good habits and suppress great faults, compared to others who cannot do this well. And always having them so, it stands to reason that they will have more honor and benefit than others who do not. I myself have often clearly seen this in people who devote a great part of their lives to such activities. And everyone who has been to war, and has seen and heard the great deeds that take place, knows what advantages are enjoyed in warfare by those who ride good horses and know well how to ride them. And so I will forebear to write more about it, to avoid excessive prolixity.

Chapter 2: The benefits riders receive in the arts of peace

In time of peace, those who practice this art receive great advantages in jousting, tourneying, playing at cane-games,[8] wielding a spear and knowing how to throw it, and likewise in all other equestrian arts that are widely practiced in noble households. For in proportion to

---

[8] On cane-games, see the Introduction.

the level of expertise their nature has allowed them to attain in any of these arts, their skill as horsemen gives them advantages over those who are not, even if they are equal in knowledge of the art itself and in physical aptitude.

As to making them good huntsmen, skill in horsemanship makes them better able to endure great encounters,[9] proficient and judicious for striking well, strong in their saddles, knowledgeable in maintaining their horses well, and capable of getting aid from them when and as they should, and of guarding against many dangers. All these, and other things that will be explained in Part III, are essential to know if one wants to be a good hunter.

This art helps them look good on horseback, and because they are seen to be good horsemen, lords will tend to assume that they are good in actions of war and other good arts, which is of considerable value, and others will esteem their opinion as regards keeping good horses, knowing how to ride and correct them well, and maintaining good and well-mounted horsemen in their household, which are things that most lords value.[10] It can also help squires, wherever they are, demonstrate that they can readily perform an art that brings them esteem and recognition as men ready for action and as worthy servants, presuming the other characteristics are reasonably evident in them.

Chapter 3: What might be said against the benefits of this art, and the rebuttal

You should not heed what some people might say against this, that many are good horsemen, but are little valued for it. This art by itself is not sufficient to make someone valuable, as are other skills by which men live, unless you happen to be a horse-dealer or want to breed and train them. For the principal things that (with the grace

---

[9] *Encontro* (Sp. *encuentro*) is the Iberian term for the impact between opponents jousting with lances; Duarte may here be thinking of using a spear in the "couched" position while hunting, as he discusses at length in his section on hunting below.

[10] Piel divides this sentence differently, but the meaning and manuscript layout suggest the above reading.

of God) allow men to acquire good things in this world and the next are these: to have a good will to do all things virtuously and faithfully to God and to men; to have good and reasonable strength of body and heart, by which we have the power to enact, counteract, and endure all major events and adversities; and to be knowledgeable through experience and natural understanding regarding things that pertain to our estates and offices, which will allow us to know surely and truly what we should desire, enact, counteract and endure, both within ourselves and in external actions. These are the virtues that are sufficient by themselves to bring real benefit to people who have them; other arts are not, except to the degree that they are accompanied by these virtues. But he who lacks these three things should not expect to be good at riding, jousting, dancing, or any other art that can greatly benefit a knight or squire; he might well succeed as a craftsman or jongleur. The more a knight or squire has these three principal virtues, the better he is; and those who have them are often helped by some of these lesser arts. And everyone should work to know much about them, according to their estate, age and natural disposition, considering the great benefit and enjoyment they can often derive from them if they know how to use them in accordance with the appropriate manners and occasions for doing them.

Chapter 4: The enjoyment that arises from this art

It stands to reason that those who excel in this art should have much enjoyment, given that we see people who excel in arts of little profit—such as throwing the bar, jumping with feet together, and other similar arts—enjoy praise for their excellence.[11] If these people naturally rejoice in such praise, what should someone do who excels at the art of riding, which enjoys such a privileged place among the people to whom it pertains? It is also generally recognized that good and agreeable mounts greatly please their riders' hearts, if they know reasonably well how to ride them. So to conclude what I said at first: anyone who sees these benefits and pleasures that arise from this art,

---

[11] These sports are described at length by Monte (*De Dignoscendis Hominibus*, chs. 9–19; *Collectanea*, I.19–29, II.129–40, 147–48).

and many others that one could discuss at length if it were necessary, would have great cause to desire it.

I have written so much about this topic to induce those who read it to have great will, for if they have it, they will easily find the ability and knowledge they need in order to be good horsemen.

In sum, a man who has good mounts and knows how to ride them, receives these [seven][12] advantages:

> First, to be more ready to serve his lord and help in the various situations that can happen to him, for his honor and benefit.
> Second, to enjoy riding.
> Third, to be honored.
> Fourth, to be protected.
> Fifth, to be feared.
> Sixth, to be cheerful.
> Seventh, to develop greater and better courage.

You should understand that such a man has these benefits much more than those who have bad mounts or are not good at riding them, presuming they have everything else equally to experience these benefits.

This art is also excellent because a healthy man who has a good and resolute will, and is not too fat, will seldom or never lose it, as happens with most others. And if someone has a good manner of bearing himself excellently, it will always make him look good when he is riding a horse or any other suitable animal with appropriate training.

Here ends Part I, concerning the Will, and begins Part II, concerning Ability

Chapter 1: Ability of body and of means

As regards the sufficient ability that horsemen should have, it is divided in two parts: one is physical aptitude, and the other is means.

---

[12] The text erroneously reads "six". This is not the only place where Duarte is careless with numbers, cf. below p. 78 fn. 28.

Concerning the body, some people think they cannot be good riders because of weakness, old age, or obesity, and therefore lose the will and give up learning what they need in order to attain knowledge. They are manifestly quite wrong in this, and in many other good things that they lose because of this despair, when they could acquire them if they had good hope. Those who feel this way ought to dismiss this belief. They should reflect that they feel badly because they don't think they can acquire this art; but if it is due to weakness or age or some other thing, they could easily find others who are weaker and older but are quite good riders. Likewise with the other shortcomings: most people can recognize that, even if we have them, we can find others who have them to the same degree or greater, yet are not prevented from having considerable skill in riding. And when we see that people of equal or greater shortcomings acquire this art and practice it quite adequately, we should readily recognize that, if we have will and knowledge, the ability will not fail us, since people can do it who have less aptitude than ourselves. I truly think that if everyone believed this, few people would fail to become reasonably good riders for lack of physical aptitude. By "good" I do not mean "excellent," because I believe that in every country one finds very few people who have all the skills that the outstanding rider should have, as I will explain in another section.[13] But it suffices that on horseback they should look and act like men, and not like animals less useful than the ones they ride.

Chapter 2: Ability of means

The ability of means is divided in two parts: first to purchase and possess good mounts; and second to maintain them. For both of these, as long as we have great will and much knowledge, few of us will lack the ability. Gamblers find what they need for gaming, and drinkers find enough to spend on fine wines, and so on with other unbecoming arts that are of no benefit to lords—indeed they ban or censure them. So it stands all the more to reason that you need not lack in this one, if you have a resolute will. There is no expense for

---

[13] It is not clear that Duarte ever wrote the material referenced here, though perhaps he is referring generally to the contents of Part III.

which you might ask your lord for subsidy with less embarrassment, than to buy yourself mounts and maintain them, nor any in which lords are more generally willing to oblige.

Knowledge greatly assists ability, in allowing you to get a better bargain in purchasing foals and other animals that can be had cheaply. If we are knowledgeable about them, we can purchase and raise them, and benefit from them, which others cannot do if they do not know how. It also helps with maintenance, for someone who has the knowledge and will can keep a mount much more cheaply than others who lack good knowledge.

I do not intend to speak about how to maintain mounts in summer and in winter, how to make them robust and keep them that way, or the knowledge of illnesses, breeding, and training when they are young, since these are discussed at length in various books of veterinary care.[14] But if someone has great will and knowledge about all this, as long as he is not unlucky in mounts, it stands to reason that he will always be better able than others to keep and maintain them.

Part III, offering Sixteen Chief Recommendations for the good rider

I have now finished the first two parts: Part I offers some reasons why knights and squires should have great will to acquire this art; Part II discusses the ability of body and means, which most people have sufficiently. I will now write Part III, offering such recommendations as can be written, regarding the great knowledge that I have said is necessary to be good at this art. Some of these things cannot really be expressed in writing as they are practiced and demonstrated to the sight, so if you cannot understand what I write, I advise you to ask people who you see are knowledgeable about it, for such people can instruct you in what you cannot teach yourself.

---

[14] No veterinary treatises are listed in Duarte's library inventory (Duarte, *Livro dos conselhos*, pp. 206–8), though numerous treatises were in circulation at the time he was writing; on medieval veterinary literature, see above p. 34 fn. 65.

And for this you should know that a good rider should have the following properties:[15]

> The first and most important: you should hold yourself strongly on the mount in everything that it does or that can happen to it.
> Second: you should have no fear of falling from the mount or falling with it, in moderate measure as one ought to have such fearlessness, according to the person, mount, place, and what you have to do on the mount.
> Third: you should be confident in will and in comportment of your body and face in everything you have to do, and know how to show your confidence.
> Fourth: you should be firmly seated in the saddle in an appropriate manner, as required by the nature of the mount and what it is doing.
> Fifth: you should be fluid in everything you have to do; and in this matter I will briefly offer, as best I can, instructions on certain arts that are done on horseback.
> Sixth: you must know well how to strike with the spurs, as required by the situation and by the mount; and regarding this I will write about the design of spurs, and how you should govern with a stick or rod.
> Seventh: you should hold your hand well with all types of bits and horse's mouths at all times.
> Eighth: you should know how to guard against the hazards that arise from falls and collisions with trees, men and animals, which put many people in danger owing to lack of knowledge.
> Ninth: you should know how to traverse the ground well in scrubland, mountains, and hills, and every other kind of place.
> Tenth: you should be very judicious in everything you have to do on horseback.

---

[15] The following list lays out Duarte's plan for the remainder of the book, although only topics 1 to 6 and topic 8 were actually written.

Eleventh: you should be elegant in every kind of saddle and style of riding and in the things that the mount does, as required by the saddle and style and what the horse is doing; and you should know how to configure yourself and your mount to look good and show well, and to conceal shortcomings in yourself and the mount.

Twelfth: you should have good endurance in going on long journeys and doing great runs, with little labor for yourself or your mount.

Thirteenth: you should be good at recognizing horses' mouths, and in having bits of all kinds made for them, according to what is needed.

Fourteenth: you should recognize horses' shortcomings and faults, and know how to eradicate or amend them.

Fifteenth: you should know how to recognize, maintain, and increase a horse's good qualities, not worsening them through disordered will or lack of knowledge.

Sixteenth: through experience and general rules you should recognize which horses are apt and good for every purpose.

There are more things that a perfect rider ought to know, which are discussed in books of veterinary medicine; but to avoid prolixity, given that others have written about it, and since I do not myself have such great experience as in the matters I have just listed, I do not intend to write about them; but if you consult books on these matters, the more you learn, the more you will be a greater master in this science.

[Section 1: Strength]

Chapter 1: On being strong on the mount in everything it does or that can happen to it

I have said that one of the main things you should possess to be a good rider is to be strong in holding yourself on the mount. For this purpose you should know that you can help yourself with these six things:

First, by having a good manner of riding upright on horseback and in everything you do.

Second, by tightening your legs.
Third, by firming your feet in the stirrups.
Fourth, by holding on with your hands at the moment of need.
Fifth, by knowing the manner of riding that each saddle calls for, according to its style and configuration, in order to be stronger in it.
Sixth, by knowing how to configure yourself, the saddle, and the stirrups advantageously for whatever you have to do, as required by the manner of the mount.

We need to know how to assist ourselves well with all of these things, but not equally, nor at all times, nor for every mount. For the principal and most general ones are: knowing how to sit upright according to the things you are doing; tightening your legs; helping with your feet and hands; knowledge of saddles; and configuring yourself, the saddle, and the stirrups.

Chapter 2: "Brabant" saddles

To better explain what I have just written, you should know that generally there are five distinct ways to ride, from which all the others are derived.

First, there are those saddles that require you to have your legs straight and a bit forward and firmed in the stirrups, sitting in such a way that you are relying equally on all three parts, not placing greater emphasis on firming your feet than on tightening your legs or sitting in the saddle, but taking equally from all three the good assistance that you can and should have from them. Among the saddles that are used in these regions, the ones that principally call for this kind of riding are the ones that today are called "Brabant" saddles, and others of similar design. If you want to ride strongly in a saddle of this type, you should extend the stirrups so that you settle in it, holding your legs straight. Yet you should not do this so much that it makes you lose the force of your feet, nor should you firm your feet so much that you loosen your legs. Rather, as I have said, you should envision being equally helped by all three parts, without being more firm in one than in another.

Chapter 3: Styles that do not pay great attention to the stirrups

The second style involves sitting fully in the saddle, holding your legs straight or a bit gathered, not paying heed to the stirrups, so that your feet are mobile in them. I am told this manner is used in England and some districts of Italy in the saddles they use, although they are of various fashions. In this style the strength of riding lies in keeping yourself upright and tightening your legs, according to the moment, always sitting upright in the saddle, not paying great heed to the stirrups. Yet as it seems to me, in spite of the fashions of the saddles and style of riding they require, you should not entirely disregard the help you can have from the stirrups, even if you devote more attention to tightening your legs, keeping yourself upright, and knowing how to hold your body in everything the mount does, rather than to the help of the feet.

Chapter 4: Styles that ride firm and high in the stirrups

The third is to ride firmed in the stirrups with your legs straight, not sitting in the saddle, but receiving some help from the arçons. The saddles in which you ride this way are the ones in which we once used to ride in this country, and those in which we joust or tourney, and others of similar fashions. The way to ride well in such saddles is as follows. You must make the stirrups firm with bindings or strong straps, or some other good manner. You should not thrust them forward, and your legs should always be as straight as you can hold them. Your feet should be quite firm, and you should never sit in the saddle, because it makes you lose elegance, fluidity and steadiness, and also makes you less strong. You should not suppose that to be stronger in the joust, it is advantageous to sit in the saddle with one of your legs gathered, because certainly the reverse is true if the stirrups are bound; rather you should do your best to hold both of them quite straight at all times, for it often gets us out of mishaps and falling, and makes us more fluid and elegant.[16]

---

[16] Gathering one leg when jousting probably refers to the jouster flexing his left leg in order to brace it against the saddle, to counteract the impact coming from that direction.

Chapter 5: Riding with gathered legs

The fourth is to keep your legs gathered, sitting in the saddle with your feet firmed. Everything here is the same as I have said for Brabant saddles and others that call for that style of riding, except that in these you should never be stretched out, while you should not be gathered in Brabant saddles. And these are the jennet saddles and others that call for this kind of riding. The firmest way to ride in these is to squeeze your feet and the whole of your legs right up against the horse as much as you can, keeping them gathered, and riding in the middle of the saddle, not sitting against the rear or forward arçon. Your feet should be well firmed and flexed, as if the stirrups were attached to them, lowering your heels, and entirely observing the manner I have described, not sitting carelessly in the saddle such that you loosen your legs and fail to firm your feet. Nor should you firm your feet so much that you rise from the saddle or loosen your legs, but you should tighten them in such a way that you keep your feet fluid and mobile in the stirrups. And you should tighten your legs equally at the calves, at the knees, and above, so that everything is as evenly tightened and firmed as possible.

As to sitting in the middle of the saddle, you should understand that this applies if the horse is running or walking. If it is jumping, it is good to stay in the middle of the saddle, firming your feet and tightening your legs, and straightening your body backwards, as I will explain when I discuss how to keep from falling forward. If the horse is trotting, the best way is to hold yourself firm on the rear arçon. If it is cantering,[17] or trots poorly or hard, you should lift yourself in the stirrups and come against the forward arçon.

In all the saddles I have mentioned you could observe this manner of riding with the legs bent, just as with the jennet saddle, sitting strong and settled and fluid, but it is not elegant in others that I have seen, only in jennet saddles, in which to my mind it looks good when people ride this way when they have occasion to use them.

---

[17] See the Introduction on the gaits.

Chapter 6: Riding bareback or on a pack-saddle

The fifth manner is riding without stirrups, using a pack-saddle or entirely bareback. The trick here lies in tightening your legs and holding yourself upright. And there are three different versions: first, with the legs extended and tightened at the knees and thighs; second, gathering the legs and squeezing them against the horse; third, squeezing with the entire leg this way, and placing the tips of the feet near the mount's elbows.

Chapter 7: The benefit of knowing all these styles of riding

All other manners of riding are based on these five. In this country I see riders use all these styles, some in good and ordered manner, in keeping with the type of saddle, the activity, and the nature of the horse; others, not knowing more than one manner, try to ride the same way in every kind of saddle. But if you want to be a good rider, you should know as much as you can about all these ways of riding, because you will often need to ride in each of these kinds of saddles, owing to breaking of a stirrup, or because you find the stirrups too long or short in a situation where you cannot adjust them, or because you find yourself in saddles of various types. If you are unaccustomed to more than one type of saddle, and you should happen to be engaged in some valiant action, but in a different type of saddle, you will not be half a man. Many who are called riders quickly realize that, if they break a stirrup, they cannot and dare not undertake any risky activity without great danger; others who know how to handle it will not find it a great inconvenience. I truly believe that if a Marinid from Fez were in a Brabant saddle with long stirrups, he would not be a strong or fluid rider, even if he was reasonably good in his own style of riding.[18] Nor do I think an Englishman or Frenchman would handle himself well in a jennet saddle with short stirrups, unless he had some practice riding in it beforehand. Likewise with everyone who knows only a single manner of riding: finding himself in another kind of saddle, he will be half crippled. A good rider does

---

[18] The Marinids or Beni Marin were the Berber clan who had ruled Morocco from Fez since the 1200s. Ceuta and Tangiers were both part of the Marinid territory.

the contrary, for in time of need, he is not so inconvenienced by the saddle or stirrups that it hinders him much in what he needs to do, compared to the great hindrance that others experience.

Chapter 8: How it always helps to ride upright in everything the mount does, and how we can fall in each direction[19]

To hold yourself strong in all these manners of riding, it is always principally necessary to know how to ride upright in everything the mount does, as I have said, and to recognize how to help yourself and what you should do. Other things can also help, as I will explain.

Keeping yourself upright should be understood as follows. We can be thrown off the mount in one of four directions: forward, backward, or to either side. We can be thrown forward by the following situations: when the horse baulks, or when it bucks, landing back on the forefeet near where they were before, which some mounts will do deliberately, or throwing the hindlegs and placing the head between the forefeet after bucking, running in some other disordered manner, or in doing even an easy jump, if the mount has the habit of jumping on the forefeet, suddenly throwing itself down in a ditch, furrow, or some similar place, or tripping, even if you have the mount reined in, and halting on the forefeet when it is running.

We can be thrown backwards by rearing, bucking, jumping, just at the beginning of a run, ascending sharply in a very steep place, or in a very thick spot where some brush interferes with us and the disruption makes us fall.

We can fall to one side or the other when the horse shies to the side, turns hard, slips the shoulder, when it bucks, throws a kick, or beginning to baulk, deviating to either side.

We can also be thrown in each of these four directions by some external force, or wielding a spear, throwing it, cutting with a sword,

---

[19] The density and technical subject-matter of this chapter make translation a challenge; some readings depend on how one punctuates the text, others are hindered by technical terminology whose precise meaning for Duarte is uncertain. The translation deliberately preserves some of the ambiguity of the original—although much of what Duarte describes will be readily familiar to experienced riders.

or doing some other thing that can make us fall if we do not know how to hold ourselves well, even if the mount does nothing to throw us.

Chapter 9: How to respond when the mount does something that can throw you forward

With all of these situations that can throw us, it is a great advantage if we know how to ride upright; for you will readily see how most men fall for lack of this knowledge. If a mount baulks on me, I need to guard against falling forward, so it will help if I put my hands on the horse's mane and lower myself, supporting myself in the direction where the mount tries to throw me. But if I do this, it is a sign of disconcertion or lack of knowledge, for in such a case and in all others where we are thrown in that direction, the help of the hands is useful only as a last resort, when we are on the verge of falling. Alternatively, as I have experienced sometimes, when the horse bucked briefly and would throw its hindlegs at the end, I would throw my hand onto the rear arçon or the iron strut that some saddles have, which allowed me to keep my body more straight and stable than by putting my hands on the mane. Someone who knows this well can do it so covertly that even if he has a light stick in his hand, it will never be noticed by others unless they know the trick, as long as he is wearing the right clothing for it. I have had very certain experience of this myself, for I have tried it without having seen any other rider do it or speak of it. And I believe that if anyone wants and is able to do it to help himself, it will be profitable for him in the moment of need—for you should avoid it if you can.

If you want to protect yourself in any of the aforementioned situations that throw a rider forward, you should always take heed and, as the mount acts, tighten your legs, firm your feet, and straighten your body back as best you can in a good and reasonable manner, with your legs straight or gathered, depending on what the saddle calls for. It also helps in such cases to angle your body, gathering one leg so that it can tighten better, and the body holds itself more still and secure. Acting this way, you will never receive a jolt or unbalancing that can greatly affect you. As to throwing the hindlegs, you can respond sufficiently by firming your feet and straightening your body, without tightening your legs, if the mount has the habit of throwing them straight.

Chapter 10: How to respond when the mount does something to throw you backwards

When the mount does any of the things that can throw us backwards, people generally find the best help they can, which is to grab on with their hands and pull their body forward. But they are wrong to rely on grabbing, for you should never grab if you can avoid it by the posture of the body and tightening the legs. You should avoid it because it is not elegant, and because your hands, as far as possible, should be kept ready for use, so they should not be occupied with holding you onto the mount if you can manage without their help. But if you must grab, it is better on the mane or the forward arçon than on the reins.

Many people, when they begin a run, put their hands on the mane in order to sit firm or get steady, and once they have the habit they cannot let go of it. I have found a sure remedy for this: never running for a few days without something in the right hand, until they lose this habit. When the horse jerks forward, I slant my body a bit, lowering myself forward. This keeps the jolt from moving me backwards: I am much more firm than if I stay entirely straight, and I will have to straighten up before I can move backwards. By the time I have straightened up, the initial jolt has already passed: the horse has entered into the run, and once he is running, the rider is easily sure and steady without help of the hands.

Thus in situations that can throw us backwards, we should chiefly help ourselves with the comportment of our body and tightening our legs, and, in greater need, with our hands, but very little with our feet. I truly believe that you are more likely to fall in this situation by firming yourself up your feet than to get any real help from them.

I have also found a certain technique for when the mount ascends a very steep incline, keeping yourself upright without placing your hands on the mane: it works well to gather your legs, tightening them, and lift your feet backwards, with your body upright. This makes it seem as if you were passing over a much flatter place than it actually is, as experience will show anyone who tries it properly.

Chapter 11: The analogies that we can derive from this riding upright[20]

This manner of riding upright on horseback seems to me something that we should observe in everything we do, in order to be good horsemen in the world, and to keep ourselves strong so we do not fall because of the vices that throw many people in this manner. At times in life we encounter adversities of action, speech, care or memory, such that we feel ourselves at risk of being thrown into rage, ill-will, sorrow, weakness of heart, demeaning ourselves, or giving displeasure to God and men, or we are preoccupied by lack of faith or despair of our ability to begin, continue or finish well the things that we can and should do; or we are thrown into some trouble that comes from weakness and carelessness of will. At such times, promptly looking to our Lord God for our chief assistance, we should straighten ourselves by our own power and good counsel, and by that of others who have great knowledge and extensive and good experience, so that they have the knowledge, will, and ability to act and advise in such matters. We should keep in mind the counteracting precautions for whatever is making us fall in one of these directions, and we should always speak and hear the things that counteract the failing to which we feel ourselves most inclined, and not those that unbalance us more, even if our will desires it—sad people often like to speak of the causes that engender their sadness, even though this makes the sadness increase.[21]

If we have the will and ability to do this well with the grace of our Lord God, soon with His help we will know how to ride very upright in most of our deeds. And if presumption, pride, or vainglory try to make us rise and tumble into a fall, losing some good beginnings of soul and body that God has granted us, we should promptly present to our recollection how little we can achieve by ourselves: by recognizing our shortcomings, with His grace we will be preserved from falling into these errors. And since we do not have the chief

---

[20] This chapter corresponds to *Leal Conseilheiro*, ch. 83.
[21] Duarte's remarks on *tristeza* (sadness) are based on personal experience, discussed at length in his analysis of his battle with depression in *Leal Conseilheiro*, chs. 18–25.

power in ourselves, we should beseech help from Him who gives good beginnings, so that He will allow us to continue and finish well. And even if we do not quickly feel the improvement we desire from such counsel, we should persist, and we will see before us the great benefit that we will have from such discipline of will and care.

If we begin to do something with good intent and foundation, and human malice, necessity or chance get in the way, we should not let this stop us from acting uprightly in accordance with the matter and as required by the due execution of our own estate: we should never hesitate to carry out what we ought to do, nor should we hurry in the effort and work beyond what is good. But, as matters proceed, with secure will and without perturbation, we should do whatever we see is required by the time and situation. By maintaining this manner in our life, with the help of Him who grants us all good, we will always ride upright and cheerful in all our actions.

It may seem excessive to pursue such a discussion here, since it digresses from my main topic, but I have done it to benefit some readers, even if it is not very pertinent to others.

Chapter 12: How we should act to avoid falling in each direction

As I have said, whatever the mount does that can throw us in any given direction, our most important help lies in moving our torso, neither hesitating nor rushing such that we turn our body before the mount, or stay behind as it turns or swerves. Rather, to cultivate knowledge, confidence, and good habits, our body should match the horse: if it turns with the forefeet high and hindlegs low, we should ride with our body somewhat leaning forward; if it turns on the forelegs, with the hindlegs high, our body should go upright, leaning back as called for by the height of the hindlegs, neither delaying nor rushing, but matching the horse. Doing it this way, we can be sure not to fall or experience any trouble. To do this it helps greatly to tighten our legs, with our feet and hands assisting when necessary.

Chapter 13: Where it is best to tighten your legs, and how you should bear your feet

Returning to our topic, some people question whether it is more secure to tighten the legs at the knees, or above, or at the calves; and whether we can sit more firmly with our whole foot in the stirrup, or the middle, or just the tip. To this I respond[22] that none is better than the other, for I have seen strong riders use each of them. To ensure strength, everyone should ride as he is accustomed and as called for by his saddle and stirrups, and the things he or the horse is doing. Tightening the legs more in one place than in another, or having the whole foot in the stirrup, or not so much, makes no great difference. We can well see that riding strong in a jennet saddle involves tightening at and around the knees and below; the rider derives a great part of his strength from the heels or spurs, and virtually nothing from the knees upwards. Those who ride in a Brabant saddle receive great help from the knees upward. Those who joust in our manner are principally helped by the knees and around them.

The same thing applies to the position of the feet, as we can see by experience every day: some people do it one way, others in another. Generally speaking, most people find greater strength placing the entire foot in the stirrup. And regarding this you should know this precept: if we want to have our feet entirely in the stirrups, to be more stable in the stirrup the tips should go a bit outward; and if only to the middle or the tip, we should turn them inward. Anyone who tries it will certainly verify what I have said. I do not need to offer any more discussion because this is enough. I am not saying that in each of these styles the tips are far to the outside or inside, just a slight difference. This is how to be strong; to look good, I think people will say it is better to keep the feet straight, not pointing in or out, according to our custom.

---

[22] *A esto eu respondo*: This is the technical legal formula for introducing the approval of laws in the Cortes, and reflects Duarte's experience with legislation in his role as crown prince and later as king of Portugal. On the Cortes, see Duarte, *Livro dos conselhos*, pp. 171–72.

Chapter 14: The advantage of knowing the manner required by every type of saddle

The things I have just written make it clear how we can and should help ourselves by how we hold our body, tighten our legs, and firm our feet, using our hands as a last resort when other means fail. I still need to explain the help that we receive from knowing the manner of riding that every saddle calls for, and from the configuration of the saddle, the stirrups, and ourselves. As to the knowledge of riding in each type of saddle, you can clearly see how much we can be helped by what is written above concerning the manners of riding, where I said that the jennet style calls for having the legs gathered, and sitting inside the saddle. Someone who had never seen this, and was accustomed to ride in other saddles that call for extended legs, stretching them out as in a Brabant saddle, would never ride as strong as someone who was accustomed to hold their legs gathered, as such saddles require. The same applies to all other manners of riding that I have mentioned, for it is certain that a man will never be a good all-round rider if he does not know the best manner for every type of saddle. And given what he knows of various types, when he uses a new type of saddle, he will know how to recognize the style of riding it calls for.

Brabant saddles also call for different manners depending on their design. Some are high and strong in the rear and front arçons, and short in the seat. If someone tries to ride in this kind of saddle as he is accustomed, he will never do it well, for its tightness does not let you stay seated in the middle, when the mount acts roughly. In such a saddle it is better to lift yourself in the stirrups two or three fingers above the middle of it, holding your legs straight, and observing all other specifics as described above. If the saddle is long or flat, it is best to sit in the middle of it, although not in such a manner that you lose the force and help from firming your feet and tightening your legs. And as I have said, when jousting in our manner, where you are strapped in place, it is much stronger to be high in the stirrups than inside the saddle. But if you are not strapped in place, it is better to sit in the saddle than to ride lifting in the stirrups. Thus each type of saddle calls for its own style of riding, even though the differences are minor.

Chapter 15: How to take care of the saddle, bit, and all the other appurtenances so they are strong and properly adjusted, and do not break or shift

We must help ourselves by properly adjusting our saddle, bit, and stirrups, firstly making sure that everything is strong and so well secured that we cannot receive death, injury, or shame from any of them failing, as happens to many people. This requires us to check them often and diligently, and to correct whatever is wrong, promptly and without hesitation or cutting corners. If someone is charged with correcting it, and fails to do what he is ordered, or what he should attend to, he should not escape without amends and punishment, for there is nothing that pertains to a mount's equipment or care that should be looked after with greater attention.

In this matter you should observe a precept I received from the king my lord and father (may God keep his soul). He said that even though something seemed very small, if it could bring us dishonor or great loss in body or in means, we should attend to it as if it were a great matter; contrarily, if the matter seemed large, but the most that might arise from it would not entail great loss, we should not pay great heed to it. This can be exemplified in everything we do.

But returning to our topic: suppose I find a horse cared for so poorly that for lack of care it could die, and I see the bit broken, and my groom could easily see this if he looked; but for the lack of care no other harm could happen but loss of the horse or not looking so good, while from the broken bit I might undergo any of the things mentioned above: for the lack of care I should give him a moderate penalty or punishment, and for the bit a much bigger one.

Chapter 16: The configuration of the stirrups and stirrup-leathers

You should take great care that the stirrups are neither very wide nor very narrow. In wide ones the feet do not stabilize well, and in narrow ones they hurt and tire more quickly, and they are very dangerous if the foot gets caught and cannot be pulled out of them. The tread should be neither very thick nor very thin, for on thick ones the foot cannot flex well, and on very thin ones it hurts and tires, and for some people it can lead to a cramp. The reasonable measure for most stirrups seems to be from two fingers up to two and a half,[23] in the case of French ones. For jennet saddles, even though others have various opinions, I prefer them light, more on the small side than large, not broad, and such that the feet can catch and release them without impediment.

I have found a new way to fashion covered stirrups for jennet saddles and for all other saddles. In my opinion (and I have extensive practice with them), they are very beneficial for holding the feet, and they make you ride more strongly; in falling you come out of them more easily; and they have other advantages that are easy to recognize if you try them.

The stirrup-leathers should be broad, but such that they can readily pass through the stirrups, and strong, such that they sit still. If you have to ride a spirited mount, the saddle-flaps should be such that they do not move under your legs; for I have seen some people get into trouble for not knowing how to handle this, riding on saddle-covers of cloth or leather, or having them so poorly and weakly adjusted and of such a style that they shift around; and so they should be very firm. These days I see some people in Brabant saddles pass their stirrup-leathers below the saddle-flaps; this strikes me as a good custom that makes them ride more confident and steady.

Chapter 17: The configuration of the saddle

The saddle should have its saddle-tree, arçons, and all other fittings such that they will not break or become disordered. It should be made such that the rider receives help from the front and rear arçons. The place where the legs go should be suitably concave. The saddle should not be long in the seat nor too short, for in a long one a man is unsupported, and in a short one you cannot comport yourself well. And everything should be arranged according to your own style, the style of the saddle, and what you have to do in it. You should avoid having anything that causes annoyance, like rear arçons that curve too sharply to the legs; or a forward arçon that turns in very high, or is insufficiently concave where

---

[23] Approximately 1½ to 2 inches—Duarte is clearly referring to the front-to-back measurement.

the legs go; or being poorly adjusted in the latigo, girth, rings, and stirrups, in such a manner that any of these things feels as though it is unsatisfactorily made or adjusted. For a rider certainly endures great discomfort if the saddle is made or adjusted contrary to what he would want and should have.

You should ensure that it is well placed on the mount, according to the manner it requires: some mounts need to be saddled more forward, and others more to the rear. Also, a saddle may be well padded in the front or the back. Anyone who rides in it will find it beneficial to be well informed and have everything adjusted to their advantage, particularly on active mounts. If it has the habit of jumping on the forefeet, or throwing the hindlegs, it is certainly a great advantage to put the saddle forward, touching the withers. For just as we see that ships labor less near the mast, so mounts that do these things are felt less when they bear the saddle forward. If it does this on the hindlegs, with the forelegs high, it is better to have it somewhat further back. I have recently had saddles made in a new style, with the rear arçons turned, low at the concavities for the legs; they offer greater advantage than one might think to look at them, and are quite comfortable for traveling on a long journey.

Chapter 18: About our own outfit and how it should be

We will receive help or discomfort in riding from our own outfit—the spurs, gear, style of jupon,[24] overgarment, belt, and what we wear on our head.

Our footwear should be tight in the middle of the foot, with the toes slender, a bit long, comfortable, and without a long tip. If it is

---

[24] The jupon was a close-fitting jacket worn over the shirt. It served a structural purpose, since a man's leggings were typically supported by being tied to it with laces (also called "points"). Over the jupon there would normally be a looser overgarment of some kind. The belt would be normally be worn outside the overgarment, serving to arrange the overgarment stylishly and to support a belt-pouch. The structure of clothing during Duarte's period is described in Forgeng and McLean, *Chaucer's England*, pp. 117–55; see also Davenport, *Costume*, pp. 293–302. On Portuguese male clothing of the period, see Marques, *Sociedade Medieval*, 23–54; Marques, *Portugal na Crise*, pp. 466–70.

very slender, and broad in the middle, the foot will hurt and will get tired more quickly. If it is short, hard, or tight in the toes, or has a long tip, the foot will be unable to flex well or firm itself in the stirrup.

The spurs should have strong irons, fittings, and leathers, and they should be positioned correctly. When they are this way, sometimes we receive great help from them. The length should be suitable for the saddle in which we are riding, and what we have to do.

We should be equipped in such a way that all our legwear is close-fitting, for it will make us ride more steady and firm, and not loose—yet not so much that it impedes or inhibits us. If we are riding jennet-style, the legwear should be fuller and less fitted.

The jupon should be made such that it does not constrict or catch anywhere, nor should it cause encumbrance or impediment. It should not be so broad that the body is entirely loose; if it is close-fitting, it should not make us uncomfortable at the collar. If the skirt is long, we should take care that the lacing-points sit above the rear arçon when riding in a Brabant saddle, lest they get untied somewhere if the jupon is open on the sides or ties so tight that its skirt cannot pass beyond the arçon. This may seem trivial, but I have seen it give rise to great inconvenience for some riders who were attired this way.

The overgarment should be reasonably short, as is the custom, with sleeves that are light and not oversized. All riders will certainly find themselves stronger if they are efficiently and lightly clothed than if they are encumbered or wearing garments that impede them.

What I say of overgarments also applies to armor, for the lighter and more efficiently a rider is armed in whatever he has to do, the stronger he will find himself. Some people believe they are harder to shift out of the saddle if they are weighted down, but I maintain that they will find themselves in a worse position, and slower if they get off balance, so that the benefit is outweighed by the loss. As for being strong in defense, I do not deny that it can be helpful.

Our overgarments should be loose-fitted, like mantles and surcoats, or others of such fashion that they can be worn easily. If you have to wear a belt, it should be belted at the middle, and tight. If your body feels uncomfortable when it is held down tightly, you should gird yourself low and high,[25] with the belt tight enough to hold itself in place, or attached at the sides so that it does not slip.

You should not wear a great hood or capuchon[26] on your head, but a small one, or a brimmed hat: on a lively mount you will certainly find anything heavy or inhibiting on your head to be a great encumbrance.

You do not need to worry about these things for riding on every mount, but only on a mount that is very active—in that situation, whatever you try to do, you will generally find that a small factor produces great hindrance. And beyond what I write, everyone can experiment to find out what he finds advantageous. Every discerning person will certainly find great advantage in the things he has to do, if he starts by guarding against anything that can bring him injury or interference. And one of the surest forms of learning that we can acquire is from our own experience. Therefore you should observe closely, and recognize what brings you benefit and seems better; for in this and all things most men have their individual ways that they find greatly helpful or hindering, while others find it differently.

Chapter 19: How some people fall by trying to do something, even when the mount does nothing to make them fall

I have said that we can fall forward, backward, or to either side by exerting some force—wielding a spear, throwing it, cutting with a sword, or trying to do some other similar thing—if we do not know how to hold ourselves.

To explain this, you should know that most men fall in these manners through disconcertion of will. It happens as follows: if a man encounters with an opponent in war or jousting, or something comes up against him, or exerts force to throw him in any of these directions, and his will gets disconcerted, and he does not know how

---

[25] low and high: *per fundo & alto*. This might refer to buckling the belt low in front, with the strap riding higher in the back; or perhaps it should be translated as "low or high," representing the alternatives of belting below or above the belly; cf. below, p. 72 fn. 24.

[26] capuchon: *carapuça*: Terms for specific garments are often used loosely in medieval texts, but given the context this may refer to a large stylized hood wound around the head, as was fashionable in the fifteenth century.

to hold himself as he should, most people will certainly fall owing to failure of the assistance they should have from the body, legs, feet and hands. I am not saying this is true in every case: some people receive such great encounters, or are pulled or pushed so hard in some direction that they have no force or power that can hold them in place. But if they have confident and lively wills and know how to help themselves with their advantages, they will often avoid falling, nor will they receive such a jolt as will greatly disrupt them. This happens as with men who are unskilled in wrestling: any force or technique thrown at them makes them fall very easily owing to disconcertion of will and lack of knowledge.

We can see this exemplified in the life of men, for many people allow themselves to fall into evils and live as wretches, from minor contrarieties and occasions that befall them, due to weakness of heart, lack of knowledge of how to govern themselves and their actions, or because they do not teach themselves through good habits to endure these things and help themselves with good strength and counsel, whether from themselves or from others who know the matter well and could offer it.

In wielding a lance, or in trying to do other arts, many people fall this way from error of will. This happens by weakness or by excess, along with lack of knowledge. Some do it from weakness, being weak or inhibited in it by nature. When they are commanded or have occasion to do one of these aforementioned things, they are greatly disrupted, so that they fall very easily from disconcertion.

Others do it from excess of will and lack of knowledge and practice: when they want to do one of these things, they get so worked up, concentrating on doing them well, that they forget how to hold themselves on the mount, and so they fall. I have seen some people fall this way trying to wield a spear: they cling to it so hard that they cannot manage or raise it, and when it falls to the ground, they go with it. In throwing, some people are so focused on throwing far that they lose track of the mount and go right out of the saddle with the spear. And so it happens in cutting with the sword, or striking overhand with the spear, or doing some other thing: by concentrating on what they have to do, many people lose track of the mount, and fall from disconcertion and lack of knowledge.

Chapter 20: How to wrestle on horseback

Since some people grapple each other by the arms on horseback to throw each other, whether in earnest or wishing to try it in play, I want to write some precepts that are profitable for this, which I think people will find good if they practice them.

First, choose a saddle that has the kind of rear arçon on which you can firm yourself. People believe that a jennet saddle is better than others, even if it is not a huge advantage. This holds true for anyone who knows how to firm himself on the rear arçon.

Second, you should not set great store by firming in the stirrups, unless they are strapped in place; for when you want to let yourself move around as your weight shifts, you are more impeded than helped by greatly firming yourself in them.

Third, you should squeeze on the saddle with your legs. And while you are working you should never release them or neglect staying upright in the saddle, but keep steady, and work on your opponent as best you can.

Fourth, grab your opponent as high as you can, or at least by the arm, for this makes his body weight shift more.

Fifth, if you see that your opponent disregards his saddle to grasp you, take him by the arm, and pull him across to the outside. Since he is not sitting in the saddle as he should, he will be easier to throw.

Sixth, when you are working, as quick as you can, give your opponent a turn backwards over the haunches of his mount, and continue to pull him in that direction; even without great force, this can lift him or the mount, if you pull well. To do this better, at the moment of grappling, your mount's head should never stand outside, but turned as much as possible across the other's haunches.

Beyond these recommendations, everyone who tries the art can himself find other good ones, which can be of use in time of need, even if it happens only rarely. And to throw the mount, there is an excellent technique by which someone who knows it well can grab the horse by the head near the bit,[27] pulling hard, holding the hand

---

[27] *mossos*: Piel conjectures that *mossos* means mouth, but it is unlikely that Duarte would use such an unusual plural noun to describe such a common body part. Throughout the *Livro de Cavalgar* he uses the standard singular noun *boca* to

strong, and lifting the head to make the horse stumble and fall. Those who are well advised, proficient on horseback, and reasonably hard and good riders, can help themselves with all these advantages—for others cannot take such good advantage of them.

Chapter 21: The manner we should observe when we have to do any of these things or other similar ones

When we do any of these things, our will must be sure, and our principal intention to remain upright on the mount, so that in doing them we never concentrate on them to the point of forgetting to stay on the horse. If we are wielding a spear, we should devote more effort to tightening our legs and holding ourselves firm in the saddle than to the strength of the hand or arm to support the spear. If we cannot do this with the spear, we should drop it, and keep our body steady and secure, and not try to do more than we can achieve, holding ourselves straight on our mount as we should; in letting it fall, we should never abandon the good manner we should observe. Likewise in throwing we should principally focus on firming our feet and tightening our legs and holding ourselves firm. We will help ourselves as much with this attention to the hand, arm and body as by our skill at throwing. And we should do the same thing in cutting with a sword or striking overhand with a spear, never losing track of the saddle for anything that we have to do. If we practice such a habit, we can turn it into something that comes naturally. This is a good precept and very profitable and elegant for anyone who knows how to do it.

We can well take example from this of the various ways for men to live. Some people are unmindful of the good and upright lives required by their place in society, and fix their intention hard and heedlessly on doing what they want, even though it is a thing of little

> refer to the horse's mouth (ed. Piel, pp. 77, 88, etc.). As Piel also notes, *mossos* is etymologically related to French *mors*, suggesting that Duarte is referring to the mouthpiece of the bit; cf. also *morso* in Grisone (*Art of Riding*, p. 543). The technique of yanking on the bridle to throw horse and rider is attested in other sources (cf. Tobler, *Captain of the Guild*, pp. 314–15); some bits were garnished with spikes to counter this technique (Fallows, *Jousting*, p. 246; Zschille and Forrer, *Pferdetrense*, pl. 10 no. 10; Tavard, *Sattel und Zaumzeug*, pl. 66).

worth, to the point that they fall even as they achieve what they wish to do. Although it ultimately gives them cause for sorrow, ill-will, committing robberies or similar evils, they are quick to follow their desire, without any regard for what they ought to be doing.

Others, regardless of their strong intention to achieve whatever it may be, never undertake more than what they can do well, always doing what they should with attention to their consciences and role in society. This way they certainly do all good actions better, and our Lord grants better outcomes in them. And likewise when a man devotes all his principal intention to holding himself upright on his mount, as I have said, he does much better everything he has to do on horseback.

Those who practice these arts will gain solid experience of these principles. And we should not believe people who know little of these actions, or practice the contrary. For lacking this kind of practice, they will never be able to speak or advise about it. Certainly most men sometimes have cause or receive advice to pursue lives that appeal to them more, and they pursue them until in due time each receives his recompense. But in all things good men should not worry about opinions, but should follow the clear signposts on the straight road that has long been deemed worthy for righteous men, and their will should never deviate from it on account of anything that arises, trusting in their recompense from the true Lord who gives graciously to each person according to his works.

Here ends Section 1, about Strength, and begins Section 2, about Fearlessness

Chapter 1: The various causes of fearlessness, and how some people are fearless by nature

Now that I have finished writing the recommendations that seem good and reasonable to me for riding strongly, in keeping with art and good order, I will write others to help us ride without fear, as I have said good riders should. In this matter you should know that all men, greater or lesser, can be fearless in all our actions for twelve[28]

---

[28] Duarte only actually mentions eleven reasons. This is not the only place where he appears to be careless with numbers, cf. above, p. 54 fn. 12.

reasons: nature, presupposition, desire, ignorance, good experiences, practice, reason, another greater fear, position of advantage, anger, and special grace.

First, some people are fearless by nature, because they were born without fear, shame, or reasonable inhibition, whether in most actions, or in some particular ones. And as the saying goes, "Whatever nature grants cannot easily be taken away." Also we see some men fear the dangers of battle, but endure fearlessly those of the sea; others cannot face battle or travel at sea, but are utterly fearless amidst great plagues. Some have great shame or inhibition in doing certain things, so that they would rather endure some great danger, than do them in a public place, for fear of public blame or embarrassment it will bring them. Others have no shame to do them; and so on for the various characteristics that each person receives naturally at birth.

Regarding this, you should know that we can err through insufficiency, not being adequately and appropriately bold in the things we do, or by excess, having more natural boldness than is reasonable, without fear, shame, or inhibition. Since we can err by excess or insufficiency, virtue will be found in the middle, as is written of true strength: it removes fears and tempers excessive boldness, helping us to dare rather than to fear.

Speaking here of what everyone receives by nature, I believe that as in other things, there are some people who are naturally fearless riders in a proper manner, acting in accordance with what is called good nature, which desires things of the nature and degree that it can govern well. In situations where they should be bold, they are as bold as one ought to be, and with things that should be feared, they fear and guard against them as is reasonable. It seems to me that we see a very clear example of this in mastiffs, even though they are animals who do not possess reason. Some, being excessively ardent by natural inclination, throw themselves down from houses, pass through fire, and do other follies. Others, who fall short, are so extremely cowardly that they dare not try any doubtful thing. And some are so temperately bold that they fear what ought to be feared, and where they should be fearless, they are as much so as the boldest.

What happens with fear in this respect can also be seen with shame and inhibition. I make a distinction between inhibition and shame. Reason makes us feel shame for things that we fear we have done badly, or for what we are doing or will do, when our understanding judges that we do badly, or we think we might be faulted for it. In this respect we can exceed by having too much shame, or fall short by not feeling it in those situations where we should; or we can have it in good and reasonable manner as I have written concerning boldness, as long as we have it with good temperance.

Inhibition pertains solely to the feeling of the heart, which cannot judge rationally whether the thing that engenders it is good or bad. We often feel it in situations where we actually recognize it is bad for us, and would very much like not to feel it. But in my opinion this can only happen through the help of the good fear that comes from shame, feeling it when you should feel it, which protects us against such things when the feeling arises through the perception of reason. By itself inhibition is of no value, and everyone should free himself from it as much as he can by good sense, practice, and each of the things that remove fear, for it is no help, except in the aforementioned case. Many people are fooled, hearing people praise the fear of shame, which comes from the proper recognition of things and from the virtue by which we fear to fall into such error, so that it is proper for us to have it. But thinking that this is the same thing as inhibition, such people conclude that inhibition is a virtue, when it is actually a fault that everyone should remove from their heart and will as much as they can.

I do not mean to offer more advice or instruction on these matters, for they are natural characteristics that we cannot amend except by recognition of reason, and by the other things that I have already spoken of. Where they come into the discussion, I will write what I think about them. But I have written this to offer what seems to be necessary background for what I am writing, and so that every reader can recognize in himself how he is naturally inclined. And although it is said that we cannot change things of nature, I believe that, with the grace of God, thanks to good understanding and general good will, men do amend much in their natural shortcomings, and increase in virtues. Therefore each of us should work to understand himself, and to maintain and foster the virtues that we naturally receive, and amend and correct our shortcomings.

Chapter 2: How some people are fearless through presupposition

The presupposition that one knows how to do something well allows many people to do it without fear: it is said we do not worry about things we know we have learned well. Everyone can see that if he knows he can do something well, he does it more fearlessly than something he is unsure how to do. This is not contradicted by that which often occurs, when we are more fearful of something we know better than of another that we know less. This happens because of other causes among the twelve[29] I have listed: the presupposition of knowledge cannot diminish fear to the point that some other cause might not make it grow more due to what has already been experienced in other situations. But other things being equal, to the degree that someone recognizes that he can do something well, he enables himself to do it without fear. In riding as in everything we wish to do, if fear impedes us from doing something well, we should strive to learn it. Once we know it, we will have a good opinion of ourselves in it, and soon all or most of the fear will vanish.

Chapter 3: How desire makes some men fearless

Some are fearless in their actions through desire, as we all know well. Hence we have the saying that nothing seems impossible to someone who desires it greatly. This is so obviously true, that I might readily be excused from writing more about it. But to continue as I have begun, I will write what I have learned.

Everything that we do by will is to achieve one of these four ends: pleasure, profit, honor, or honest purpose. We say that something is done for desire of an *honest purpose* when it pleases us to do it purely for love of some virtue, not having our principal intention on any other profit, honor, or pleasure that could arise from it, but only because we know that what we do is good, without having our principal intention on hope of recompense that we might expect from it.

Principal intention means this: suppose a lord rewards his followers for doing what they ought to do, without concrete hope of any other benefit that he expects to receive for it; aside from this intention for

---

[29] Cf. previous fn.

which it is principally done, he recognizes that he will be more loved and better served for doing it; yet even though he knows all this, he knows that his heart's main motivation is the desire to do it because he knows it is good: this is what we may call the principal intention. When something is done with that desire, we may say that it is done for an honest purpose.

We desire things through all four of these desires: some for good intention, some for the contrary, and some for an honest purpose that is untouched by sin or reward. In each of these cases, great desire certainly helps greatly to remove fear. And seeing that for desire of gain mariners do not fear the perils of the sea, and public thieves do not fear justice, who can doubt that, if someone had great desire to know well how to ride, this desire would not make him lose the fear of falling from or with his horse, so that no impediment could keep him from becoming a good rider?

Chapter 4: How ignorance makes some men more fearless

Concerning how some people are fearless due to ignorance, we have the saying: "A seasoned bird fears the snare." Ignorance is divided in two parts: one pertains to understanding, the other to the feeling of the heart.

As to understanding, we recognize dangers through those that have already occurred, evaluating what might happen in relation to what we have seen and heard. Based on this evaluation, we fear the harm that could happen to us. This also happens based on what we know has taken place in one situation, extrapolating to what might happen in another, even though they are not the same. The fear that arises from this source is never a fault, for reason always teaches us to do what is beneficial to us, and to fear the contrary. If we fear what we should not fear, certainly it is not because of reason, but due to lack of knowledge of what is good, or not wanting to do something that we properly understand. And even though we see some people who lack understanding and are bold, and others, who are called sensible, who fear excessively, I say that ignorance does not make boldness a virtue. To be virtuous, the work itself must necessarily be good and done in a proper manner: it must be done deliberately; we must work to the best of our knowledge; and we must feel pleasure and delight in doing it. This applies in all manner of virtues, aside from strength, where we cannot have the enjoyment in doing dangerous things during the battle, before the victory is complete. If someone is fearless where he should be, I believe he will work in that action more judiciously than an expert who, by force of fear, does not recognize what he should recognize, or who knows it, but whose heart teaches the opposite of what is good because it lacks proper strength, owing to its fear or anxiety.

In relation to the role of reason, it is good for us to know what is dangerous in the art of riding, and what is not, even though it may seem so, so that we can fear the one, and not worry about the other. For in all actions, anyone who knows them well will fear the real dangers more, and will receive little impediment from things that seem dangerous but are not.

As to the role of the heart, it recognizes and comes to know dangers principally from things that happen, either over a long time, little by little, or suddenly due to a single event. Without such knowledge it does not fear, and if it experiences intensive adversities, it comes to fear what it did not fear before, unless the other causes help it not to feel such fear. This is how it would be if a person who had never experienced fear took part in a battle in which he was injured but came out victorious: the knowledge of the injuries would make his heart fearful less than the good outcome of his victory would increase his daring to engage fearlessly in another battle. The same could happen through any of the other things I have said can make us lose fear. But by itself, the very ignorance of the dangers in which we stand, or which could follow, often makes people not feel fear.

It is good to guard ourselves from such knowledge of the heart by always doing what is reasonable. Therefore in riding we should recognize common hazards, so that the heart does not have to learn them at its cost. For once it receives an intense experience of something, it often develops such fear as will seldom or never be eradicated. But if we learn to recognize hazards through instruction, with the grace of God we will be protected against misfortunes, and in the things we understand by reason, we will develop the daring we ought to have, and will fear as we should.

Chapter 5: How good experiences make some men fearless; and how to teach boys and others who are starting to ride

It is so clearly known that good experiences remove fear that the matter does not require much discussion, for experience shows it clearly enough. Hence they say that a taste of the game meats makes the hounds lose fear. And one of the good experiences that can foster good horsemanship is to have good and well-trained mounts at the outset, depending on the stage of the student; for those who are beginning to ride should have of one type of mount, and another at the later stages.

Since we are speaking of this, you should know that to teach a boy or someone else who is just starting this art, at the very beginning he should be given a very healthy mount that is free of vices, and it should be well adjusted in the bit, girths, stirrups, and saddle. You should not give him instructions except to stay tight on the horse's back and hold himself well however he finds most suitable. Whatever he does wrong, you should not correct him much, but minimally and gently. If he does well, you should praise him generously—as much as you can without lying. You should continue this way with him for a time until you see that he is coming to enjoy learning and practicing, and wants to receive correction and teaching. From then on start explaining to him how to hold himself strongly, for this is most necessary, always minding what I have said: more praise, less blame. If he happens to fall, or loses a stirrup, or some other contrary thing, and you see that he feels it greatly, you should excuse it as much as possible, so that he does not lose the hope and will that is of great value for this and all other things.

You should make him practice riding frequently on the mount, and not too much at one time. Have him run, and jump some easy jump that will be safe—the most I have in mind here is a bar or a large pole lying on flat ground. Have him jump this, taking the horse to a canter, and advise him well of what he should do, as I have written. Have him do this on such a mount until he loses all fear. When you see that he runs and jumps on this horse without fear, find him another that shakes itself and hops, as frisky little horses do, and have him ride that horse most of the time. And you should not let him ride much on mules or hackneys, or other mounts that people ride for ease or safety, for it will impair his will and he will not want to return to others once he is accustomed to these. But he should practice with all types of saddles, hunting and hawking, and wielding and throwing spears.

By wielding a light spear that he can handle, he can be taught to maintain good manner and comportment. Likewise by throwing something reasonably light, he will better develop the technique of throwing. You should never allow anyone who is inexperienced to throw anything that is sharp at either end, for it has one end to enter the ground, and the other to injure whoever throws it, and one can receive great harm from it. Therefore to learn this art safely it is good to use a reed or a staff rounded on both ends, of reasonable weight according to the boy's size.

Once the boy shows himself strong and fearless practicing these arts on such mounts, you should once more provide him with good mounts, and make sure everything is as well adjusted as possible. Since he already has strength and daring, he is at a good point to learn everything else a good rider should have, and any error should be corrected strongly, as often as it takes until he has learned. And while he is practicing on good mounts, sometimes he should ride others, to experience vices that are not dangerous, such as being excitable, turning to the hindleg,[30] and other similar ones, and also horses that are very wilful. Also have him run without stirrups, and try other similar things, to see what can happen to him. For I do not recommend that proper men should try things in which there is manifest danger. Anyone who has the good fortune to have such mounts and teachers will have an experience that will greatly help him lose fear in this art.

There are other experiences in war, jousting, and tourneying through which riders greatly lose fear. And since I believe most experiences that present themselves to human reason happen chiefly by the just ordinance of our Lord God, we should work first and foremost to have His grace, and thereafter the will, knowledge and

---

[30] It is uncertain what Duarte is referring to here, but it could be the tendency of some horses to turn back toward the rider's foot to express impatience.

ability that I said at the outset are necessary for all things. If we persevere in this, all experiences will come to us by His just ordinance as is best for us.

Chapter 6: How practice makes some men fearless

Practice makes all men more fearless, if they are not hindered by any of the other causes I have already mentioned. Hence they say that things we practice do not give us trouble. And coming to our topic, you should know that if we lose the practice of riding willful and restless mounts, and running and jumping in reasonably challenging places, then fear, inhibition, or shame will make our will fear to do it, so that, if we leave it for a long time, we will find ourselves noticeably lacking the courage we once had. Therefore if someone wants to possess this art well, never for estate nor age, to the best of his power, should he let fear or reluctance make him lose the reasonable practice of riding mounts that run and jump, lest his heart begin to feel such fear. If he loses the practice, over time he will develop more fear, and it will make him lose a great part of this art.

Chapter 7: How reason makes men fearless

Some men are without fear in some things because their reason shows them that it is not good for them to have it. Hence they say that quarry of the hunt are ruled by nature, and proper men by reason. This is not true of everyone, because only a few govern themselves by ordinance of reason, and most by desire of will. The distinction works like this: some have such scant knowledge that they do not recognize what is good or bad, or their will is so rigid that it obscures all reason or strength, even if it cannot completely blind them. Others, who are good, always rule themselves by reason. These people must often do things they do not want, and avoid doing what they do want, as their good and proper understanding dictates: they will do nothing without its permission, just like well taught boys, who will undertake nothing without permission of their tutors. If someone has this custom, when he sees he should not have fear, he will certainly lose most of it, even though it may be present on account of any of the other causes already mentioned.

Therefore it is good for knights and squires to know how much advantage arises from this art of riding, so that they will not fear to undertake and practice it. In order to attain the benefit that can arise from it, and avoid the shortcoming of not knowing it, they should force their will to practice it, and not allow themselves to lose it after they come of age. For with most men fear comes from running and riding on willful mounts, and if reason does not come to their aid, they will largely cease to practice it; and the more they avoid it, the greater fear they will have and the worse they will ride, as I have said already. But recognizing the harm that could follow from this, they should compel their will always to maintain the practice and daring that their understanding tells them they should have. For as most boys are less worried about falls than they should be, so men always fear them more than they should. Boys typically need to be advised to be circumspect and keep their running moderate in some situations, but as one advances in years, one needs to use reason to develop the strength and custom to avoid becoming cowardly.

Chapter 8: How some men are fearless on account of some advantage, and how men become fearless through some other greater fear

Because some men see they have an advantage over others, they act more fearlessly in those things. This can come from strength and knowledge in arts, from the arms and help of men and mounts, and many other things, depending on what everyone can sense in himself and recognize in others. Hence it is said that a person fights more fearlessly when he knows his back is covered by the support that he provides himself or expects from someone else. Therefore it is always very beneficial for everyone to work to have as many good arts as he can, as I have already said. For someone to lose fear of riding in this way, it is best to use good equipment and good mounts, for this fosters daring, and the contrary increases fear.

It is clear that men can lose fear in some instances by some other greater fear. Some people in ships, fearing the power of the sea, let themselves be broken on land, and others, fearing fire, throw themselves down from houses. Hence it is said that a great worry removes other lesser ones. If someone fears the shortcoming of being a knight or squire who does not know how to ride, and recognizes that if they have fear or inhibition to try it, they will never know how to do it, this fear will naturally make them lose most of their fear of falling, with the mount or without it, so that it will not keep them from becoming good riders.

Chapter 9: How some men are fearless due to anger

It can be readily seen how anger makes many people lose fear of some things, which they would have without it. Therefore some people debate whether anger is good for people, since it helps in this respect. Setting aside many reasons that one might allege on one side or the other, based on what I have learned, this is the clear conclusion: for a good man it is entirely superfluous, since his good understanding and just will, along with temperance and strength, suffice him for living properly and doing what he should. Anger may be good for this man in some things: it depends on whether he feels it against himself when he does badly, or against someone else in a case where he should not.

As to others who are more weak and gentle in some things than reason properly requires, anger is very good for them as long as it is not so great that it hinders them. But if it makes them do what reason commands, as they would not do if it did not compel them, it is very profitable for them in such cases. So returning to our intent: if some knight or squire does something wrong on horseback, and recognizes that he has committed the error through not knowing how to ride, and becomes angry with himself, it stands to reason that he will work to learn something of this art that he did not know before, and would not were it not for this anger. By this example we can see for whom anger is beneficial, and how one can use it to overcome fear.

Chapter 10: How some men are fearless by special grace

Obviously in order to have any good art or virtue, we need the special grace of our Lord God. Nonetheless, in this particular case I say this: if some man generally in his actions fears more than he should, and finding himself in some dangerous enterprise he shows himself so fearless that it brings him honor and allows him to avoid great harm—what would we say did this, if not special grace? Likewise we see some people who are fearless in all their actions, yet sometimes they fall into great deficiency and dishonor. What can be said of this, but that God for their sins specifically deprived them of the great benefit that had been granted to them? Recognizing this, we should work, with His mercy, so that at times of need and necessity we do not forfeit the good grace that He gives us in riding and all other things, but rather we may see that He grants us more.

I have written at such length on this matter because I well know that many people have greater fear than they should in riding and other good actions, and end up lacking knowledge of things that they could do well, and would be profitable for their advancement and great honor. When each of us recognizes the causes that can engender this fear, and how we can improve, by the grace of our Lord God, with some good strength and knowledge, it stands very much to reason that we can improve more quickly and better in what we do than if we do not understand or know how the fault comes to us, and the things that can help us deal with it.

Here ends Section 2, about Fearlessness, and begins Section 3, about Confidence

Chapter 1: Explaining the ways one can acquire confidence

Being fearless in riding gives us great cause to be confident in will and comportment, and to know how to show our confidence. Nonetheless, owing to some of the causes already mentioned, a person can be without fear, yet not confident in will, nor able to show their confidence. For example, if someone undertakes to do something on horseback, when because of melancholy his heart is not free of all fear, shame and inhibition, even though he has lost enough fear to be able to do it, he will still certainly neither show nor possess the good and proper confidence that a good rider requires.

Among the things that I have said remove fear, there are four that most principally engender this confidence: nature, presupposition, practice, and reason. Since I have already spoken about how nature, presupposition, and practice make us lose fear and acquire confidence, I will proceed to show how reason helps in having, maintaining and showing it.

You should know that lack of confidence of will manifests itself in these five ways: fearing to do something; doing it hastily; being disordered and awkward when one does it; rising slowly and hesitantly to what one should do; and visibly putting greater effort into it than one should.

Chapter 2: How one shows lack of confidence by fear and by haste

To explain this better, I will offer an example. If someone riding on horseback fears danger or shame, his will is certainly no longer confident: fear is in his heart, and even if he also possesses confidence, both cannot really remain in him at one time in relation to the same thing. If he has fear of what he is doing, he cannot have confidence as long as the fear lasts. Even if someone gets up the courage to ride a wilful mount, through anger or the other causes I have written about, or undertakes to do some equestrian activity in which he is not fully confident, his fear will quickly be evident through his face, body, or comportment, for anyone who has good knowledge of the art.

Lack of confidence can easily be detected in the form of haste, for when someone fears something that he sees could harm him, he hastily wishes to remedy the situation. Therefore it is a well recognized sign that someone lacks good confidence of will in an action if he hurries in doing it. But you should not conclude that he does something with haste, if he is doing it with proper eagerness. For there is a great difference between them, according to this distinction: eagerness makes us execute without delay whatever our good and proper understanding commands us to do, while haste comes from the heart, manifesting a general haste in all one's actions, due to fear of something, as is written above, or having excessive will in it. And usually it makes us do poorly, always showing lack of confidence.

Chapter 3: How disorder and awkwardness show lack of confidence, and how acting too slowly in doing what we should shows the same lack

Things that are in the heart cannot be perceived by others except through externally visible actions; therefore when we see someone who delays greatly in doing something he should, we say he is not really confident in it. When someone hurries because he is naturally hasty, we may conclude that he does it without proper confidence, if it is such a thing as could cause fear, shame, or inhibition, even if he does it thanks to his natural condition; likewise when we see that he comes slowly and hesitantly to what he ought to do in the work he does, if it is such as could cause the same feelings, we quickly fault him for not doing it confidently, even if he does this because he is naturally hesitant or slow.

Chapter 4: How you can show lack of confidence by doing something with more effort than you should

Speaking properly, anxiety or fear is contrary to confidence. Therefore when someone shows in his manner that he puts more effort into what he is doing than is required, it clearly demonstrates that his heart is not very confident: fearing some contrary thing that could come to him, he puts too much care into it. When we see him do it this way, we quickly conclude that he lacks confidence. And one could demonstrate, before the action and after, that fear and anxiety are in him at both of these stages.

I will offer an example on our topic: if someone is told that he will be riding a willful horse, and he, fearing danger or shame, does not dare to do it, clearly he shows that he does not have a confident will in that action. If we see that he corrects himself in riding in a manner that is hurried, disordered, or awkward, or delays more than seems reasonable, we would well say that he does it for lack of confidence. And if all he has to do on the horse is make it run, or jump a moderate jump, and we see that he puts excessive diligence into correcting himself, to keep himself from falling, we would judge that it is due to lack of confidence. In such a situation we see the rider respond to any small jolt by tightening so hard and hanging on with such comportment that it instantly reveals his shortcoming. Likewise in other similar cases we can readily recognize how many failings are revealed by doing things with a greater show of care and effort than the action really requires.

Chapter 5: How one can acquire and demonstrate this confidence

Having stated and explained the things by which one shows lack of confidence, we can easily recognize how confidence should be acquired, maintained, and demonstrated, for by guarding ourselves against the contrary, we gain what we wish to have. For example, if someone recognizes that he lacks confidence because of his fear, shame, or inhibition in riding, he should heed what I have written above where I explain how people can lose fear, and do as I have written, and I believe he will acquire enough confidence to suffice for this action. Setting aside all the others, simply by having practice on good and well-trained mounts, according to his personal qualities, we can be sure that he will receive great improvement.

Concerning what I have said about disorder, awkwardness, and haste, and devoting greater effort than is required, everyone can tell whether he errs in any of these respects. For if he does not recognize his own shortcomings, he can never really improve himself in this or anything else. If he sees that he errs by haste, he should do it for a while so slowly that it feels as if he is acting more slowly than he should. Likewise in the others, where he detects a failing, he should practice the contrary to the point where it feels a bit excessive.

For this is a general rule: when we wish to straighten a crooked stick or staff, we bend it in the opposite direction, and we should do similarly if we see that we are not keeping to the middle in some virtue, falling into error at one of the extremes. As quickly as possible we should throw ourselves for a while in the opposite direction, so that by this practice, and disuse of what we previously followed, our reason can recognize and[1] our heart can possess the straight state we should have in that virtue.

When we mean to do something on horseback, if our heart does not want to pay appropriate heed owing to overconfidence, the

---

[1] [and] not in Piel, supplied from MS, fol. 111v.

desire for our health and well-being should not permit such excessive confidence, compelling the heart to pay heed to everything it should. Conversely when this desire urges me to put excessive diligence into protecting myself from the dangers that could befall me, my heart will not consent, feeling that others could blame me for it. Between these two contraries that frequently arise in each of us, proper understanding adjudges what we should rightly follow, not entirely satisfying the excessive confidence that the heart wishes to show, nor the self-interest that desire wishes to protect. We should recognize on one hand that, since we have reason, all our actions should be ruled by it, and we should not leave things to chance; and on the other, we should recognize the limitations of our knowledge and ability, and that however much we look after ourselves, all our protection is chiefly in the hands of the Lord. This way we will have temperance and not hesitate to do everything that pertains to our estate, age, and disposition, in keeping with the example of our peers whom we know to be good, knowing that the principal burden of protecting us belongs to Him who each day guards us from countless dangers. Therefore, never abandoning the practice of reason, we will take heed in all things as best we can, not ultimately relying on our own strength, but on God; yet we will not therefore fail to do what we should in all things, even though they may be dangerous, when the occasion reasonably requires it of us.

By these examples I believe I have explained how men through proper understanding can possess and demonstrate their proper confidence by recognizing their shortcomings, and mastering themselves as much as they can, and continually practicing the good manner that they truly understand they should observe in everything.

Chapter 6: How we can show confidence by certain displays

We can also show this confidence by certain artful displays: not only do these help the external appearance, but, when we practice them repeatedly, our heart becomes more confident each time until it comes to acquire the good and true confidence this practice requires. I will offer a few of them by way of example.

When you are on a wilful horse, or want to do something doubtful, you should always show good, cheerful, and steady comportment, although not so excessively that people will recognize it as fake—for if it were recognized as such, it would show lack rather than abundance of confidence.

Another: if you are rearing, jumping, or wheeling around, or if the horse is acting roughly, sometimes bring your hand deliberately to adjust your hood or belt or clothing, to make it look as though you are more focused on this than on trying to stay firm, showing that you are hardly worried about anything the mount is doing. You should not do this very often, nor repeatedly do one thing, but now one, now another, as best suits your style. And you should not do any of these for very long, only as required for what you are pretending you need to adjust.

Another way to do it is this: as you ride along, engaged in conversation with some person who is not of great account, squeeze the mount with your legs, or gently touch it with your spurs, in such a way that it is not perceptible, or tug at the bit to make it act up, making it look as if the mount is doing it. As you do this, continue speaking and listening as you were before, making it look as though you want to settle the mount, while secretly giving it reason to continue. This way, as you speak with some gentleman, you can make it look as if the mount is acting up, while you continue to show proper comportment in listening and speaking regardless of what your horse is doing; and if you are listening or speaking with someone on foot, be sure to lower yourself a little toward him, as you would if you were sitting still. Similarly when everyone around you is looking attentively at something, and the horse is restless, even though it is being quite rough, you should keep looking as the others are doing.

From this we can derive a general rule: whatever the mount does, whether it is at our pleasure or at the animal's, we should make it look as if it is all the same to us (even though it may not be), always making it appear that we neither notice it nor let it perturb us, any more than if we were at a walk.

I could give many other examples, but whoever heeds these well will see the manner you should observe in similar cases. The key to all of this is knowing how to do everything so that you always make it appear to be done with real rather than fake confidence.

Chapter 7: Concerning doubts about these displays

Some people might say that such displays should not be done by good men, because we should never use falsehood or fake displays, whether in play or earnest: we should be transparent and truthful in our actions and words, and by using such lies we could develop the habit of lying in other things, and once we get it by habit, it is very difficult to eradicate.

To this I respond that when such displays are carried out for a good purpose, for a man to train his heart well and protect himself against problems, without giving rise to other ill effects, it is not a lie, and can be done without blame or impediment of conscience. This practice will not give a good man the habit of lying in matters where he should not, for even if he does such displays, he will still always avoid those that would entail sin or real blame.

Here ends Section 3, about Confidence, and begins Section 4, about Steadiness

Chapter 1: How a good horseman should match his steadiness with what his mount is doing

I have now finished with the first three topics: first, strength, which is the most important thing for a rider to have; second, fearlessness; third, confidence. All of these are very helpful for riding well and for other things.

I will now write the fourth section, on being steady, which I will keep brief. To acquire the steadiness that you should have in the saddle, it helps greatly to have the principal elements I have just named: to be strong, fearless, and confident. But I should explain how you may develop it.

Some people think that great steadiness shows lack of fluidity, since they do not know the situations and times when it should be used. These people are quite wrong: in fact, good steadiness is very helpful to fluidity, as I will explain below. In this regard you should know that, as I have said, a good rider should match his steadiness with the work the mount is doing. If it is at a walk, it does not help or look good to steady yourself deeply, extending your legs and showing very firm and still comportment. Acting this way shows that you have fear of the mount, or that you are feeling awkward. The proper manner that you should observe at such a time is to show a general fluidity of the entire body, as confident as if you were walking on foot—not in such a way that you abandon yourself in the saddle, for that always looks bad, but, observing the comportment required by the saddle you are using, you should show your fluidity and that you are neither fearful nor inhibited. All this can be done in such a way that you keep the proper steadiness that everyone should have according to who he is, the situation, and the mount he is riding. When you trot or walk briskly, it looks better to show more firmness and steadiness. From there onward, the more the mount is doing, the better it looks to be still and confident in the saddle.

Chapter 2: How to develop steadiness

Steadiness should be generated chiefly from the knees upwards, such that you are never loose on the horse if it does something where steadiness is called for. Your feet should be quite firm in the stirrups, always in keeping with my practice, as I have written where I speak of various ways of riding that saddles require according to their design.[2] If the mount runs or acts roughly, your face should be calm and confident, and you should not move your head around needlessly, yet in such a way that you do not seem to be feeling awkward. When it suits you, or when you want to look at something, turn your face to see it with as little awkwardness as if you were doing it on foot. Secure your body by drawing your shoulderblades together and poising yourself, while remaining ready to straighten or turn in any direction, never moving around on account of the horse, but only to be in control of yourself so that you can position your body to make yourself stronger and more elegant on the horse, and with the surest and best comportment that seems good to you.

To wield a spear, or throw it, or do some other thing, your body should be so firm that regardless of what the mount does you can release your feet to strike it; and your hands should be ready for the spear and reins and for all other things, whether in armor or not,

---

[2] See above, III.1 chs. 2–7.

without awkwardness, as if you were doing it on foot, or as if the mount were at a walk.

Steadying your feet well in the stirrups, so that your feet do not shift around in them, greatly helps the general steadiness of the entire body. This calls for the stirrups to be properly equal in length. If you like to keep your feet deep in the stirrups, you should make the stirrup-leathers lie along your legs, adjusting them to a length where you can keep your heels reasonably low. And you should not use your feet where you should use your legs.[3]

If you like to have your foot in the middle of the stirrup, you should hold your heel a bit low, and thrown outward, and the instep always well poised, for from there one generates a large part of proper steadiness. Having your saddle and stirrups well made and suitably adjusted is of great benefit for this.

Chapter 3: Further explanation of how to maintain good steadiness and the benefit it brings

Drawing the shoulderblades together and poising the body makes horsemen run courses very smoothly and more elegantly. You should also learn how to strike with the spurs, for you should move your legs only from the knees downward to strike the mount. As to the arms, you should see that they are not poised with the body such that moving them makes you lose steadiness: in bearing the reins and in everything else you do, your body should always be still, balanced, and straight. Take help from your hands, arms and feet as it suits you, not moving your body more than necessary when you do so.

This manner is very helpful for keeping your armor still on your body, so that it does not shift around, as happens with some people who do not know how to poise their muscles, causing it to move around so much that it greatly impairs their elegance and fluidity. Also they are never as firm in the saddle (being of equal disposition in other things) as those who know how to steady themselves and their armor. Good steadiness on the mount helps us greatly to

---

[3] Port. *non façom do pee perna*. This probably refers to an unskilled rider trying to stabilize himself by wrapping his feet around his horse's flanks, rather than by tightening his thighs.

sit in the saddle with firmness, ease, and elegance, and to hold our hand well, and most other things a good rider should do. Those who wish to achieve this should work hard to acquire good steadiness of body, face, and comportment, and be aware of how they should act in everything, taking example from those whom they recognize as knowledgeable, and who are justly praised above others in this art.

Here ends Section 4, about Steadiness, and begins Section 5, about Fluidity

Chapter 1: About being fluid and fluidity of will

Adhering to my initial order, I should discuss the fluidity[4] you should have on horseback, the name of which at least partially explains the concept. Being fluid shows that you have none of the impediments that many people have in such a situation. These are inhibition, weakness of the disordered will, shame, lack of physical ability, limited knowledge of the art, and lack of practice. I believe it is necessary to discuss each of these, to show how we can do something to rid ourselves of them and acquire the proper fluidity we need for riding.

Some people experience impediment in their will, which greatly hampers them in what they have to do, owing to inhibition, weakness and inordinate shame. I have already discussed how we can do something to remedy this. But to explain more fully, I have seen some books describe a virtue called greatness of heart:[5] it is said that this virtue makes a man believe himself able to do everything as a proper man can and should do. This belief needs to be true, for if someone has a good opinion of himself and is worth little, we would call him presumptuous. If he is actually better at it than he thinks, or would be if he applied himself to it, then he is said to have a small or weak heart. Someone who has this virtue must have the proper self-esteem to do great and good deeds according to his person, and must act in keeping with his own self-opinion.

---

[4] See the Introduction on this concept, *soltura* in Duarte's original Portuguese.
[5] Aristotle, *The Nicomachean Ethics*, Bk. 4 ch. 3 (pp. 93–9); Cartagena, *Memorial de Virtudes*, pp. 369–411.

Since (as the Philosopher[6] says) it is difficult to have a perfectly balanced knowledge of our own selves, it is more appropriate for someone with a great heart to presume somewhat more of his own ability than to have less confidence in himself. And if someone has this virtue, presuming it is general in all of his actions, he will do everything with fluidity, for anyone will be greatly hindered in their will if they think they are erring in what they do. But those who expect to do things well receive little hindrance in their will. If they err, they afterwards make plans to rectify it, but they never hamper themselves or avoid doing or practicing what they see is good, or what it pleases them to do.

I am speaking in general terms, although some people possess this virtue in one thing and not in another, as can be readily seen: some are comfortable at riding, and not at dancing; some at fighting, and not at singing; and so on in all other matters. But if someone has it especially concerning the thing he is doing, it certainly gives him great help in doing it with fluidity.

Many people are greatly hindered by inordinate shame due to lack of good understanding, practice, interaction, advice, or attention. This reflects the distinction I have drawn between shame and inhibition. Inhibition comes from the heart, and it obstructs everything, even things we know are good to do. Shame comes from reason: if someone thinks an art is not appropriate for them, they avoid trying or practicing it, and this breeds inhibition in them, not being able to have that good fluidity that one should have in it. If this belief is in error, the error arises on the part of reason, and shame brings them inhibition.

When we want to gain fluidity of will, we must eliminate inhibition by practice and by presupposition of our ability, which involves doing as others of our estate do, holding a realistic opinion of ourselves, or better, and understanding that it is enough to ride well and

---

[6] I.e. Aristotle. It is unclear exactly what Aristotelian source Duarte has in mind here: it may be related to *De Anima* I.1.420a10–11, where Aristotle says that it is thoroughly difficult to attain any sure belief about the soul; but Aristotle was known to medieval scholars through a plethora of derivative works, not to mention those falsely attributed to Aristotle, so the reference may not actually derive directly from anything by Aristotle himself. I am indebted to Noel Fallows and Edward C. Halper for assistance with this recalcitrant allusion.

to do everything on horseback like our peers. And you should not imagine that such a presupposition should make us disdainful and proud: even if we hold such an opinion, someone who is good and virtuous will always show due honor and courtesy toward others.

Reason dictates that we should have good knowledge of the arts that each of us should use according to his age, his estate, and the situation. Even if our heart wishes to baulk, we should compel ourselves to do the things we ought to do, in order to free it from inhibition, shame and hesitation, and to acquire extensive and good practice of the art, for this greatly fosters fluidity.

Chapter 2: Concerning physical disposition, knowledge, art, and practice

Concerning physical disposition, in riding as in other arts, some people have knowledge, others have great advantage generally in all things, or particularly in some. This does not happen in a manner that can be perceived through visible signs, for some people look as if they were awkward, yet do everything easily, and others the reverse. I believe the ordinance our Lord God laid down in this matter should greatly encourage men to focus their intention on attaining whatever art they will, and not despair of acquiring it, even if they do not think their constitution is disposed to it. For they will see others who appear no more suited to it than themselves, but who have adequate fluidity in the art they wish to acquire. I believe that people fail to acquire arts more for lack or weakness of will than for disposition of body, although certainly some people are such outstanding riders by nature that few can equal them, and others are so awkward that it will take great effort for them to acquire good fluidity.

But leaving aside things that are innate, and speaking of what relates to learning, you need to possess fluidity in these four parts:

> First, the right arm, to wield, throw, cut, and do everything else.
> Second, the left hand and arm, to bear the reins and to slacken, tighten and turn them in whatever direction you find necessary.

Third, the legs, from the knee down, to strike the horse when and as you should.

Fourth is the comportment of the face and the body, as I have already written where I spoke of confidence.

The fluidity of the arms and legs calls for them to be independent of the body, with each one doing its individual work while the body remains at rest. This is one of the good habits the rider must have. And those who know how to bear their bodies with good steadiness acquire it better than others, as I have said.

Chapter 3: About some arts that are practiced on horseback, concerning which I will give further instruction below[7]

To have good fluidity, you need to have good knowledge of the arts, for in no other way can you attain or display it. The principle arts, in my opinion, are as follows.

First, to practice armed for war, with your armor configured as required for riding, jousting, or tourneying, having a good master or masters to teach you what to do. And you must believe what they tell you, and follow it, for in order to learn you must believe and obey what they teach you.

Fluidity is also greatly helped by hunting, hawking, and wielding or throwing spears, playing at cane games, and striking with the sword. All these arts should be practiced by those who wish to have good fluidity on horseback: good and reasonable practice is a great teacher, and without it no one can acquire any art; and even if one possesses the art, it can very easily be forgotten.

Continuing with my original intention, since it is more important to me to benefit readers than to guard against criticism for what I write, I will give some instructions in a few arts that are greatly used on horseback, for those who know little about them.

These are: carrying the spear just in the hand, at the leg, and at the neck; wielding and encountering with it; striking overhand; throwing it well and accurately; and striking with the sword with thrust and cut; for in this we demonstrate a great part of fluidity.

---

[7] See below, III.5 chs. 4–7, 10–16.

Regarding this I will write briefly about specific practices based on my experience, although naturally not about everything. If someone tries what I write, and fully experiences the art, experience will surely show him whether I am right.

These arts should not be disparaged by any knight or squire, thinking that they are unnecessary, but rather everyone should strive to know about them, not setting them aside as trivial, thinking they can disregard them, or believing that they are so daunting for some people that they cannot hope to acquire them well. To disparage the things that seem small, and to despair of the great ones, is surely to seek reason where you should not look for it: it consigns a man to ignorance and diminished living and achievement. They should reflect that there is no reason for someone not to keep a sword constantly girded at their side, even if many people benefit little or nothing from them, but merely like to carry them because they believe that in some time of need they could be of use: likewise the heart of someone who has appropriate knowledge of good arts receives pleasure and contentment from them, recognizing that if he needs them, they can bring him great advantage over other people who do not know them well. They should also consider that many people have been and are helped by these arts in great necessities, and on account of them are more praised and held in better account for valiant enterprises by all good men.

Chapter 4: How to carry the spear just in the hand, at the leg, and at the neck

To continue the teaching of these arts, you should know that the spear is carried in the hand in four ways: one with the arm fully extended, at the level;[8] the second a little higher and crossing over the horse's mane; another thrown over the left hand or arm; and the other at the waist, or just below or above it, held against the rider. In all these manners it is necessary to know how to balance the spear as it requires.

---

[8] Duarte may be describing a position with the arm downward and the spear roughly horizontal; Charles V is shown in this position with a light spear in Titian's 1548 equestrian portrait of the emperor (Madrid, Museo del Prado P410).

To bear the arm extended is an easy style for a throwing spear or a similar light spear. The one that goes over the horse's mane is dangerous because of the possibility of hitting trees, branches, and the like. Holding it over the left hand or arm is good when we have to encounter with the spear on that side or behind. Holding it up at the waist is better and safer for a heavier spear.

Here I am speaking of situations where you are running, trotting hard, or cantering; if you are going at a walk, you can carry it as you please. If there are trees in front, you should see that the point goes lower; if you are in scrubland, lift it up, for that is safer and easier.

The spear is carried at the leg when wearing jousting armor in a pouch attached to the cuirass or the arçon, or on the leg, according to individual custom; and it seems to me a good and convenient manner. Others just hold it on the leg, or between the leg and the arçon; those who hold it well without extra help display greater strength or proficiency.

For each of these manners the butt must be well seated and secure before the horse starts moving. We can stray by letting the tip of the spear go high or to the left, with the body leaning to the right side or backwards. To prevent this, we should do the opposite, and go as we should, that is straight and leaning somewhat to the left side from the waist upwards, and inclining forward, with the point of the spear a bit lowered and inclining to the right side.

As to the arms I make no great matter, whether holding them closed, or open and moving around more, for I have seen people use all manners elegantly enough. In this matter everyone observes his own manner or the one that seems most admired in his country. But everyone should guard against the aforementioned errors, in keeping with my practice, for I do not believe that it can look good or be advantageous to bear the spear in such a manner.

In carrying the spear at the neck, there are these errors: carrying it by the middle; with the point high; the hand next to the shoulder; straight in front of the face; or the elbow low. Whoever wants to carry it well should do the opposite: carry it by the place where he intends to wield it, or a bit forward of that, as required by the weight of the spear, the point a bit lowered, the hand at a distance from the shoulder, shifted to the outside, with the elbow high. In this manner it is more elegant, convenient and advantageous, whether in armor or without it.

Chapter 5: Instructions for wielding the spear

When teaching someone to wield a spear on foot, you should start standing in place, giving him all the instructions that he will have to observe with it, using a light spear or staff that he can conveniently manage. And they are as follows.

First, in order to take up the spear when holding it at the leg, where most people are accustomed to keep it, we should put our hand under it. When we bring it to our chest, our hand should come underarm as much as possible, flexing to act like a lance-rest, so that the full weight of the spear rests on the palm of the hand and not on the fingers.

When we need to put it underarm, we should lift it so that the butt clears the arm well as it goes underneath, and once it is there, we should make it as fast and secure as possible, resting it partly on the chest, not twisting or leaning, but keeping straight in order to breathe freely; and we should know how to do it with minimal motion of the body.[9] This helps greatly in wielding the spear without a lance-rest, because the spear is supported at three places: one at the hand that holds it up, another at the tightening of the arm that holds it in place, and third at the chest which takes much of its weight.

We should lift the spear with a sudden jolt, putting the body, arm, and hand into it, for a large spear is easier to lift in this manner than in any other. And as we jolt it away to fall from the neck, we should keep our arm well clear in the manner I have described in how the spear should be borne at the neck. If there is a vamplate, take care that it does not get stuck behind your neck, for that is very inelegant, and you can get hurt if you are not in armor.

Once someone has been sufficiently instructed on foot with a light spear, he should be taught with another larger one, and so you keep on increasing until you come to the heaviest spear he can wield. For you should not practice something you cannot do well, to avoid pulling a muscle, and injury in the lower back, head, legs, or hand, which arises from doing this carelessly.

---

[9] minimal motion of the body: *algũa pequena contenença do corpo*. Cf. below, p. 113 fn. 15.

Once you feel he can wield it well on foot, he should try it on horseback at a walk as I have taught on foot, and he should have someone to point out anything he sees done badly. For we cannot perceive our own comportment without guidance from someone else, unless we have great knowledge and practice of the art. Once he does this well, he should canter, and from there run; if he knows the art, he will find it a great advantage to ride a horse that runs hard without holding back, and has a hard mouth. It is also advantageous to wield against the wind, having it on the left side.

The spear should not fall lower than your head, but bear it at that level until you lift it, as I have already written. Do not let the spear settle hard, but take it a bit high on the chest with your arm and hand, and gently let it come to the level where you want to bear it. If the spear has a grapper or roundel of leather, your hand should be as close to it as possible, placing a finger on it.

You should wield this way with a lance-rest or without it. Knowing how to do it well without the rest, you will do it more easily with it; and in wielding the spear, observe such a manner as is described above for bearing it at the leg, placing it underarm, and lifting it up. But you should take care that the arm lifts and pushes the butt of the spear toward the elbow, to avoid catching under the rest. Once it arrives there, close it to yourself and make it settle in the rest, and support the spear high in such a manner that does not let it settle all at once, but settle it a bit high, and then bear it at such a height as you wish to bear it.

When you are wielding it on horseback, with a lance-rest or without, and the horse is running hard, in bearing the spear at the leg you should take care to squeeze your legs on the saddle and sit well. When you are placing it underarm, you should squeeze it in your hand, and do not let the point fall, as I have already said. Nor should you put it underarm with the point very high, if your face is to the wind or the horse is running hard, but get it where you intend to bear it, and there close it to yourself, steady it, and then direct it to the encounter. If you are at a canter, the best way, in my experience, is firming your feet and tightening your legs to lift your body above the jolting of the horse, and so pull the spear from the leg, set it in the rest, and place it underarm in the manner described above.

Whoever knows well how to observe this will find great benefit in doing it more comfortably and elegantly. And I will here repeat some key points, to help you better understand me—for in writing on this topic, I consider it more important to be clear than to be elegant.

If you are wielding from the neck, and you don't have a lance-rest, as you settle it, close your arm to you, and always guard against letting it settle abruptly, as I have said above. If you have a lance-rest, your arm should push the butt of the spear toward the elbow, close around it from there, and settle it in the rest. And as it settles always take heed to support it in your hand and let it settle comfortably.

There are other manners of aiming and hitting with the spear, for example on the left arm. Some people consider this way better than the other in battle, for they say that from there they can turn it more easily whenever it pleases them, and also they can better strike to that side and backwards. And when carrying it on the shoulder, if the spear is suitable, some let it fall over the right arm to defend to the rear; other times they let the point of the spear fall to the ground, and from there they return it to the shoulder and wield it.

All these manners of wielding the spear are very good to learn and practice, for they can be useful in time of need, and by practicing them we make ourselves more fluid riders. But I will not bother to write about wielding two or three spears, or spinning them above your head, because I do not consider it useful, although men who do it well display good fluidity.

Once the spear goes underarm, you can commit these errors: hunching over with it; leaning on the right side or angling greatly; riding poorly steadied on the saddle with your feet, legs, head, body, or lance; and bearing it too far across or open to the outside, or very high or low; or with your head and face arching over the spear, or very high backwards. Anyone who wants to bear it well should guard against all these mistakes, and bear it as I consider best.

Some people in jousting constantly spur the horse, shaking their legs up to the moment of encounter. This is inelegant and weakens the jouster, for during this time you should give the spurs just a few times, hard or gently, depending on the nature of the mount. And the times when you should use the spurs are these: once to get into motion, to make it enter into the canter, or to run however you would like; and again when you are steadying the lance underarm.

From there onward you should not stir your feet or legs again until the encounter is over, if the horse is going as it should—for if it shies or turns away, we should of course make it feel the spurs.

In jousting it is the custom of this region to discard the lance either to the left or the right. If it is to the left, you should give aid and balance to the unsteadiness of the body on that side, lifting your right arm well, and letting it go backwards. If you want to throw it to the right side, the best and safest way for yourself and those who are at the tilt is, as you lift it, to throw the point backward and the butt forward. If you practice both these ways, the hand, body and arm develop such mastery from it that they do it without trouble, like a good musician whose fingers work the strings, or the falconer, whose left hand knows how to do everything the bird needs, which the right cannot do, although in theory he knows it as well on one side as on the other.[10] By these examples you can see how everyone needs to have such practice of the art that the body and the limbs we must use in it may have the habits and knowledge they need.

One trick I have found when I have wielded a large and heavy spear without armor: as I lift it, before letting it fall on my shoulder, I let it run through my hand a bit. I did this to be steadier in the saddle and so that its great weight would not make me lose my steadiness; and I think that if someone were to do the same in such instances, they would derive great benefit if they knew how to do it well.

Some people can be hampered in wielding the spear even though they know well how to do it. This can be due to being poorly armored, so that the lance-rest, vambrace, or some other part of the armor hinders them; or due to the configuration of their own equipment or that of the horse; or it can be on account of being strapped in place beyond the point where they can conveniently move without trouble. So before we have to act in earnest, we should first test things, without the horse running, placing the spear in the rest three or four times, adjusting everything so that we have nothing hindering us. And even after they have been tested on a few occasions, when we actually have to use them, we should try three or four times just beforehand, placing the spear in the rest fully armed just as we intend

---

[10] falconer: *caçador* (cf. above, p. 49 fn. 5). Then as now, a falconer would normally keep his bird on the left hand.

to fight, run, aim, or joust; for this is necessary for wielding it and knowing how it will work at the encounter, as I will explain below.

If someone wants to joust in civilian clothes, he should check whether they are of a type that could hamper him, for example if they are of silk or sequined cloth, because you do not have full control of your body in them, or if the sleeve of the jupon is tight or short, or the sleeve of the overgarment[11] is made in such a way that it does not let you place the spear underarm well.

When you know that you have to wield a spear in action, look to these matters that could cause impediment; and above all make sure you have a good horse, without which all knowledge and other correction is of little help.

Chapter 6: Instructions for encountering well

To teach how to encounter well in jousting and hunting, I will write these recommendations that seem good and reasonable to me; you can extrapolate from them to every occasion this art can present.

First, in the joust, which is the most important, people fail to encounter well on account of lack of sight, failure to control their spear or horse, or failure in confidence of their will. As to sight, some fail by shutting their eyes as they approach the moment of encounter, and they do not realize it because it happens so quickly. Others know what they are doing but find themselves constitutionally unable to keep their eyes open at the moment of encounter. Others lose vision because they don't know how to arm themselves properly with their helm or shield. And some don't know how to turn their body for the encounter to gain vision, turning only their eyes or head inside the helm, and by keeping their body straight they lose vision at the moment of encounter.

---

[11] overgarment: *balandraao*. The jupon (*gibom*) was a close-fitting jacket, of a cut suitable for fitting under armor; in civilian wear, it was covered with a looser overgarment, which Duarte here calls the *balandraao*. He implies that this garment is sleeved and short enough for riding; there is no precise modern equivalent. On these garments, see Forgeng and McLean, *Chaucer's England*, pp. 131–34. Cf. above III.1 ch. 18 for a more detailed discussion of clothes.

To remedy these four mistakes, it helps to bring along someone who asks the jouster at the end of the course how he came to miss or hit; for if he encountered resolutely, he cannot know for certain. If the aider[12] sees that we do not hit our target every time, he can readily tell us what we could not see, how far we were actually off target, and that we should take care not to shut our eyes; this way we can eliminate the first mistake I mentioned above. But when a person involuntarily shuts his eyes because of his nature, it is very hard to correct.

This way, when our mistakes are forcefully pointed out, it will make us angry and unhappy with ourselves, which will help us force ourselves to change. It is also good to tell us where we are making mistakes, when we cannot recognize it ourselves. If we miss two or three times, owing to targeting late, he will tell us to target early, so that, failing to encounter by good aim, we can still encounter by chance, and if we happen to have a good outcome, the feeling of pleasure and desire can give us power to keep our eyes open in the encounter.

Bad configuration of the equipment in testing and arming can be readily corrected as follows: when we are armed at all points for the joust, sitting on horseback, we should put the spear underarm, and adjust our helm and shield such that, as the spear moves from one side to the other, holding it at the appropriate height for the encounter, we always see half of it, or at least a third, and from there forward to the end of the course. If we cannot do this, it must be corrected at once: based on my experience, I do not believe someone can encounter well if he cannot see this way. To get good vision in the helm, I consider it good to tie it first at the back such that we can see well, and afterwards to tighten it in front. This way the eyeslot of the helm is fixed more firmly and surely than if we tied it first in front and then behind.

To see well at the moment of encounter, as the opponent comes by the tilt, your entire body should be directed at him, and when you come to the encounter, your face turns toward him as much as

---

[12] The aiders were experienced knights who served as personal tutors, assistants, advisors and advocates to the aspiring jouster. See Fallows, *Jousting in Medieval and Renaissance Iberia*, p. 23 fn. 68.

possible, so that you see straight on, and not by the corner of the eyeslot. This helps greatly to improve our vision, encounter better, and endure encounters better.

As to the second principal part, regarding control of the spear, people also err in four additional ways:

> First, being poorly armed or badly adjusted at the arm, lance-rest, shield, vamplate, and grapper.
> Second, carrying a spear that is heavier than you can manage.
> Third, not being steady and fluid in the saddle.
> Fourth, riding such an unsteady horse that you lose control of it.

As to the first, a good remedy is to test things as often as it takes until you do not feel impeded or hampered by any of them when it comes time to joust. Even if you have tested it a few times, as I have said, before you come to the tilt you should put your spear underarm two or three times, keeping everything adjusted so that you feel fully master of it.

As to the second, you should never use a spear that is heavier than you can manage.

As to the third, steadiness and fluidity come through knowledge and practice of the art, as I have already written. In this case I also consider it good, according to our custom, to be strapped a bit high, with the strappings comfortable; and the saddle should be of a reasonable type, not too broad, not too tight, and well hollowed at the legs, and adjusted with good cushions and padding; and if it does not tilt backwards or tip forwards, this makes the jouster ride steady, fluid, and fully in command of himself and his lance.

As to the fourth, you should have a horse that responds to the bit and spurs, that does not rebel, baulk, or display other vices, nor should it be so unsteady that it disrupts the jouster. This can be improved by using a stronger bit, though not such that it causes the horse to rear or dip its head; and the spurs should touch it more gently, having them short and blunt. In my opinion, nobody can be considered a jouster if his footmen bear the horse by the reins, and strike it with a staff or stick: a jouster should manage the horse himself, governing by the reins and spurs, reining in with the one and striking with the other, guiding it toward and away from the tilt as he finds necessary. If you do things any other way on horseback, you can hardly control your spear and ride like a good jouster, even if a horse that runs resolutely and wears a hackamore[13] can help us bear the spear more steadily once it is in the lance-rest.

Chapter 7: Instructions for directing the horse during a joust

As to the third principal part, there are four ways that jousters fail to control their horses properly. These are as follows.

First, some people are so careless that they do not maintain any tension in the bit, letting it go so loose that they do not control the horse with it or receive any aid to hold themselves in the encounter, even if they have a *tari* bit or some other good form of bridle. Instead, they just let the footmen guide them, and once the footmen let go, the mount goes wherever it pleases.

The second use a scatch-bit, or one that lacks a curb, of such a fashion that the horses are not governed at all.

The third, to hold themselves strong at the encounter, use cords that go from the horse's face, or from the girths, passing between the horse's forelegs, and come to the rein-hand; they hold so hard onto these cords that the horses are scarcely guided by the reins.[14]

The fourth keep tension on the bit and use it to govern the horse, but as soon as the horse goes along the course and strays from the tilt, for lack of knowledge or training they do not know how to turn the horse and make it come to the tilt at the moment of encounter.

To avoid falling into these errors, you should observe this manner. First, when testing the course, take the reins before getting armored, make contact with the horse's mouth, and hold the reins where you plan to hold them in the joust. When you find a good place, give it a knot, and proceed to try out the horse. If you find it works, get armored, and hold your reins in that place. If you find any fault, whether the reins are short, long, or uneven, adjust them until you find the spot you like, and hold the reins there during the joust.

---

[13] See Introduction on the hackamore.
[14] See Introduction on this apparatus. The attachment to the headstall or girth is probably not intended as two separate physical alternatives, but two alternative ways to describe the same thing.

You can carry the reins in three good ways: some use a simple knot; others a little bar of wood attached to the reins, no longer than they intend to have it in the joust; and some give them a twist in the hand: this works nicely, and it can easily be made and unmade by the jouster, whenever he wishes, without any help. The point of the reins that should twist at the hand should have a knot positioned so that, even if the jouster undoes the turn, he can always twist it correctly, making the reins as long as he needs them. If someone forgets to bear the reins adjusted this way before he goes to the tilt, when he is at it, he can correct it in the aforementioned manner as follows: he should order his attendants not to take the horse by the reins, nor strike him, and he by himself should take the reins by the spot that feels most appropriate to him, and apply the spurs to start in motion, and make it stop, and try to turn to one side and the other. If he has a feeling for this, he will readily recognize whether his reins are long or short or uneven. Even if he has a helm on his head, pulling the gauntlet or glove from his right hand, he can adjust it himself until he finds a place he likes, and have the knot or bar positioned there as I have described. This way he will keep himself from the first error that I have said one can make in guiding the horse by bearing the reins loose and unready.

As to the second, speaking briefly, my opinion is that to do well, according to our custom, the jouster should use such a bit on his horse as guides it and suits his hand. Yet this should not be in such a manner that the mouth becomes tender or sensitive, or the horse shakes or dips its head, but the horse should be kept from these four errors, and should bear itself and turn away from the tilt or toward it, according to the will of the jouster. Anyone who does this will find he has a great advantage over those who use bridles without curbs, or bits that do not properly guide the horse.

To keep yourself from the third error, where some jousters hold so hard on the cords that come from the horse's face or girths that they maintain insufficient tension on the bit to govern them as they should, anyone who wants to bear the reins well in the joust, and has identified the place where he can make contact with them, should observe this manner: once you have found the place on the reins where you think they will work well in the joust, as I have already written, when you get into armor, take the cords and place them in your hand as you intend to hold them, by the knot or by the twist, and make a small motion backwards[15] with your body, and firm them there in such a manner that at the time of need they can help you. The reins should be so much shorter than the cords that the control of the horse is not hampered; bearing them in this way, if the jouster wants to rein in with them, he can receive great aid from them without any hindrance.

As to the fourth, in which I have said that some jousters fail to encounter because they do not know how to keep the horse to the tilt at the moment of encounter, I see people err in this matter in two ways. Some fail to maintain tension on the bit, letting their horses stray as they go along the tilt, as I have already said; others, wishing to come out best in the encounter and coming very far across, arrive so late at the encounter that their opponent passes first. To guard against these errors, you should observe this manner: as to the first, when the jouster goes along the tilt, even though it seems that his horse goes close enough, he should always make it turn its face to the encounter, and come toward the tilt as much as possible. This way he encounters better, and he and his horse will endure it more advantageously, as I have already said.

If someone fails by the other way, missing behind the helm, apparently seeking too late, understand that this error comes from bringing the horse late to the tilt; and he should take heed to come quicker, in such a manner that either he hits or he misses in front.

Since there are few jousters who know all their failings, it is a great advantage to have someone who serves in the joust to watch all these things and to identify mistakes whenever we make them, and promptly attend to them. In this way whoever follows this practice can be sure that in this respect he can conduct his horse well in the joust, which is one of the chief properties of a good jouster.

---

[15] a small motion backwards: *hũa pequena contenença de revés*. Cf. above, p. 104 fn. 9.

Chapter 8: Our four wills and how we should rule ourselves in relation to them[16]

In speaking of the confidence of will that is necessary for encountering well, I would like to indulge in a little digression of topic to offer some instruction to those who do not have great knowledge of such matters. And therefore you should know that we all have four wills inside each of us, as I have found written in a book of great authority:[17] the first is called carnal; the second, spiritual; the third, compromising and lukewarm; fourth, obedient to understanding. To clarify this, the carnal will desires physical well-being, bodily comfort, freedom from care, and avoidance of all danger, expense, and labor. The spiritual will wishes to pursue those things that appeal to the virtues. It makes people who follow the religious life pursue fasting, vigils, reading and prayer as much as they can without any circumspection. For those who engage in acts of chivalry, it makes them undertake every danger and labor that presents itself, without regard for what is reasonable for them according to their estate and abilities. It does the same thing in the pursuit of other works that seem good and virtuous, making us apply ourselves to them so distemperately that we pay no attention to food, sleep, or reasonable enjoyment that the body naturally requires. And it counsels that we should be quick to make expenditures where it seems virtuous, without any regard for what our means can cover and support. These first two wills continually argue within us, as we have all experienced: one will urges us to do one thing, and the other urges the contrary.

The aforementioned book says that between these two arises the third compromising and lukewarm will, which by wishing to satisfy both without displeasing either of them, places whoever follows it

---

[16] A version of this chapter appears as *Leal Conseilhero* ch. 3.
[17] Duarte provides the title of the book in the version of this chapter included in *Leal Conselheiro*: Saint John Cassian, *Collationes patrum Sceticorum* (cols. 593–94, 597–600); cf. above p. 48 fn. 3. See Cassian, *The Conferences*, trans. Ramsey, *Fourth Conference (The Conference of Abba Daniel: On the Desire of the Flesh and of the Spirit)*, Chapters IX and XII, pp. 159–60 and 161–64. See also Duarte, *Livro da Ensinança*, ed. Piel, p. 89, n. 3. Duarte's decision to leave the text unnamed here may be a deliberate choice intended to make the text more accessible to a non-scholarly readership.

in such a state that it never lets him live either well or virtuously, because it advises us to fast when we do not feel any hunger or thirst, and to wake when we have no discomfort in going without sleep. It wishes to achieve honor of chivalry without undergoing perils or troubles, to execute great deeds without enduring great care, and to enjoy the name of a generous person without making such expenditure as might diminish us or cause us inconvenience. In sum it wishes to follow what one will wants without contradicting the other.

The fourth will, very perfect and virtuous, does not always follow what the others call for, and often does things that do not please them, always by decision and command of reason and understanding. Hence we have the saying: "Following of will, acquiring of ill"; and to overcome this is a great virtue. This happens as follows: if a man lives according to any of the first three wills, not governing or ruling himself by reason or understanding, but only by what they want, he can expect to lose either his body or his soul. For the first will demands things so unworthy and base that soon they manifestly lead a person to fall into every evil. The second wants such high things that he can expect to come to death, madness, illness, or loss of all his property, because he has no circumspection about what he should do. The third, wishing to please both these two and bring them into harmony (which it cannot do since this is a battle that our Lord God ordains for our benefit), makes us follow virtues so coldly that it never brings anyone who is governed by it to any good estate. Hence by obliging any of these three we fall into great errors and evils.

It is very different with the fourth. Whatever presents itself to the heart from each of these three, this fourth will offers to the understanding and reason so that they may judge whether it should be done or avoided. Based on their decision, it often refuses to do what the other wills ask of it, and does what they do not want, and entirely overrules them. When goldsmiths want to know whether gold should be accepted or rejected, they put it in a crucible, and silver in a cupel, and based on this assay they reject or accept it; likewise this fourth will does or abstains from doing things based on the analysis of understanding and reason. When the carnal will wishes to dedicate itself to the things I have mentioned, the fourth will does not consent to it, but makes it suffer hunger, thirst, lack of sleep, and exposure to great dangers and troubles, expenses and cares, when reason determines that it is good to do so. It does likewise with the second spiritual will, not agreeing to follow great and high desires beyond what understanding and reason command, considering the disposition of one's person, estate and means. In this the fourth will differs greatly from the third, because that one does not wish to contradict the first two wills in any way to make them feel displeasure. But this one does not hesitate to contradict them when understanding and reason determine that it is good to do so. And in contrast with the first two wills, the fourth relies on understanding and reason to recognize what is best to do in cases where they contradict each other, as follows: when the spiritual will wants you to fast distemperately, and the carnal will, desiring physical well-being, recalls the trouble and danger that could follow from it, there is a battle and contention between them in which each argues for what it desires; and the fourth will has the opportunity to present this before the judgement of reason and understanding, and it enacts things according to their decision. This would not happen if this contention did not take place, nor does it happen in people who live so bestially that they pursue everything the carnal desire requires, entirely at its will, or in those who live presumptuously and lord it over this carnal will; nor in denying or failing to heed what it desires and fears: when we do whatever the spiritual will demands, without circumspection, great misfortunes result, of which there are plenty of examples.

By what I have written, those who are less knowledgeable can learn how we are continually tempted and importuned by these wills, and how we should not follow the first three, but all our actions and cares should be governed by the fourth, enacting and consenting to them by the decision of understanding. This should be based not only on our own understanding: where these wills call for actions in which we lack substantial and certain practice and experience, we should take counsel by the soul, body, estate and means of reasonable people, not adhering to the false belief and opinion that attracts our wills, but obeying the good counsels of others.

This is the road of true discretion, which in our language we call true sense,[18] which is greatly praised by the knowledgeable, and

---

[18] discretion: *desclição*; sense: *siso*. On Duarte's tendency toward Latinisms, see the Introduction.

which, with the grace of God, brings those who rule themselves by it to all good, and avoidance of all evil. On this fourth will true prudence establishes the foundation by which we learn to distinguish good from evil, and the greater of goods and the lesser of evils, in all our actions.

Chapter 9: By what virtues we should guide ourselves to subjugate the first three wills and follow the fourth[19]

To write as befits a treatise on riding, there are three bits that restrain us from following the first three wills and allow us to be guided by the fourth:

> The first is fear of the punishments of hell and of the temporal laws established by lords or by those who have power and authority over us.
> The second is desire of reward that we wish to acquire in this life, and afterwards in the next, by always doing good and avoiding evil.
> The third is for love of our Lord God and affection for virtues.

The first, which pertains to fear, is associated with faith in the book mentioned in the previous chapter, when we believe that, if we do evil, we will certainly be punished for it.

The second is associated with hope, by which, with God's grace, we hope for great benefits and reward if we live well and virtuously.

The third with charity, by which we love God above all things, and virtues because they please him, and abhor everything that is contrary to virtue in order not to displease Him whom we should love above all.

Although each of these virtues by itself is sufficient to guide us on the straight and narrow path that is followed by few, yet among them there is great difference. The first two pertain to those who are beginning and seeking to live in the most perfect state, while the third pertains to those who have ceased to be slaves who serve for fear of beatings, and left behind the condition of servants who always hope for reward for their good service, progressing to the state of

---

[19] A version of this chapter appears as *Leal Conseilhero* ch. 5.

good and loyal sons who hold all things of their father as their own. They serve, honor, and fear him, yet not so much for fear of punishments or hope of reward as for pure love. In this they have more continual fear of vexing the one whom they greatly love, wishing to avoid displeasing him or, by falling short, losing his love, compared with the fear of the servant, which is only felt when it is under the master's eye. This third virtue is felt continuously, for inside himself he has the great love that does not diminish from absence, but which constantly feels the presence of the one whom it perfectly loves, to guard against everything that is contrary to his pleasure. And he also has hope more abundantly, for in loving more, there is greater desire, and in desiring more, since he hopes to receive what he desires, his hope is naturally felt with more intensity.

Furthermore, when someone serves only for fear, the desire and love are free to adhere to other things, and if they increase much, they will remove him from the power of fear. If someone serves for the sake of some reward, his love is likewise free to have a greater feeling and delight in the presence of another, feeling greater love than he does for the one he hopes will reward him.

But whoever loves with all his heart, all his will and all his power, holds and keeps everything in himself. He cannot detach himself nor do anything contrary to the one he so loves, for he has great and continual fear, as I have said, and so he hopes and rejoices and delights in loving and following good will, without crossing the one to whom he is bound by such love. Furthermore, being bound by the love of virtues and the continual exercise of them serves us as a perfect bit to hold us back from all the evil and sins into which followers of the first three wills fall, allowing us to be ruled the fourth.

I have written this, even though it strays considerably from my topic, to be of help to some readers, as I have said. And what I have written calls for further explanation of these three bits that everyone should bear in his heart, so that one can feel and recognize their virtues more perfectly, beyond what I have written.

Chapter 10: How jousters miss their target owing to disorder of will, in relation to the four wills described above

Returning to my topic, jousters miss in four ways because of lack of confidence:

> First, by not wishing to encounter at all.
> Second, by tensing with fear so that they seize up at the moment of encounter.
> Third, by making the body and lance unsteady with haste.
> Fourth, by always being so eager to come off best in the encounter that they often miss.

As to the first, some jousters miss on account of a decision of will, knowing that it is good not to encounter, when they are going against someone they are afraid of, or riding a weak horse, or wielding too large a lance; in such instances the jouster decides it is more advantageous to fail to make any encounter, in order not to receive it with loss. In this way it pertains to the fourth will; and they cannot be in error unless their understanding gives them a judgement contrary to what is good to do.

Others miss owing to the first will, which I have said makes us want complete safety, and to avoid danger and effort. This is how it happens: when someone comes to joust, he intends to encounter, and he maintains this intention when he takes the lance. When he gets close to the opponent, the evil will begins to advise that it would be good to avoid the encounter, and the will that he had on the opposite side contradicts it. He continues in this contention until the moment of encounter, where the weak will often forces him to tense his body and divert the lance to avoid the encounter. When this happens, the jouster quickly gets angry with himself and plans to do better the next time. But when other courses happen, it often plays out as with the first, because at the moment of encounter the jouster's free will decides it is better to follow the advice and desire of that evil and weak will, rather than to consent with the strong and virtuous one.

It seems to me that we all usually sin this same way, when we do not fail by negligence. For before we arrive at the moment of sinning, or failing to enact some good thing that we should do, the good will remains very strong and determined to follow the better course of action. And when it comes time to execute, our free will, which previously agreed with that will, decides to avoid the imminent danger, or to pursue some pleasure that is offered by desire of that first evil will, because in this choice our free will agrees to conclude that it is better and the preferable thing to do; in this it manifestly errs, for we ourselves know it as soon as the moment passes. Therefore it is said that everyone errs either by ignorance of understanding, which does not consider or decide well before the action, or by this free will, which at the moment of action chooses the worse part, considering it better and more suitable to follow.

As to the second way, in which I have said that fear makes some people seize up, this is done by the same carnal will, but with the following difference. In the previous instance, at the moment of encounter jousters decide that they do not wish to encounter, and they intentionally divert the lance. But these, fearing the encounter as they approach it, tense themselves to get firm; and in tensing their bodies, they close their eyes, as I have said, and so they fail to encounter; or as they tense the body, they also tense the arm, making the lance go astray from its proper position to encounter. All this proceeds from the weakness of the first will.

As to those who err by haste, they position their body and the lance with the will to encounter, which can be attributed to the second will, which is called spiritual. And it happens in this manner that some foolish people in their haste cannot endure the horse's start with good steadiness, but are disrupted by the shock or jolt. And although they recognize their fault, they cannot amend themselves, because their will does not consent to it. Likewise it happens, when some good jousters joust, that they tense their bodies and move them toward the target they see, with the desire to encounter.

Those who err by always wanting to come off best in the encounter can be associated with the third will. For the carnal will, wishing to avoid all danger and effort, prefers not to encounter, and the second, which wishes to do everything that it thinks good, very boldly wishing to encounter without any prudence, are at variance with each other. From there some people come to the third will, called lukewarm and compromising, which wants to please both of these wills, decides that it is best either to encounter every opponent on the visor with great advantage, or else to miss;[20] it does this without regard to whom we are encountering, or what horse or arms we are using. And this way it thinks to satisfy and harmonize the first two wills.

To guard ourselves against all these errors that proceed from these three wills, we should resolve to govern ourselves by the fourth, obeying reason and understanding in this way: we decide what is good to do, and force it on ourselves by compulsion, demonstration of good reason, and practice.

As to the first error, because it is born entirely of will, which deliberately chooses not to encounter because of fear, we should consider what I have written about the things that make us lose fear, and help ourselves with those that most benefit us in this respect. And I think that if you desire to joust and encounter, you will there find examples and advice that will be of considerable help, if you practice it. Among the things I have said make us lose fear, one is understanding and good reason, which can be a great help as follows: consider that initial good intention that you have of encountering when you come to the tilt, and keep it in mind, and do not consent to shift from it when the opportunity arises. Also consider how few risks arise from encounters, and how many more happen in playing at cane-games, hunting, or wrestling, and that generally men take part in these sports without fear, and that we should do the same in jousting, and resolve sometimes to suffer a mishap or a fall, rather than totally fail to encounter. With such an intention, if we hold it firm and will ourselves to continue, we will necessarily encounter.

To guard against the second error, in which I have said that some men err by seizing up at the moment of the encounter, you should observe one of three ways: either the jouster should bear his lance and body all secure and comfortable, and not consent to make any other change until he encounters; or before the encounter he should tense his arm and body slightly, so that when he arrives he cannot do any more, and thus he holds until he encounters. The third way

---

[20] A hit on the helm or visor scored higher than hits elsewhere. On quantification of performance see Fallows, *Jousting in Medieval and Renaissance Iberia*, pp. 219–24. Piel here misleadingly glosses *vista* as "encounter"; in fact, it is the common Iberian term for the visor of a helmet (*Livro da Ensinança*, p. 98).

is when someone recognizes that he cannot manage either of these first two, which are better: bear the lance a little off target from the opponent, and when you arrive at the encounter, tensing your body will bring the lance suddenly to the encounter. Those who cannot keep themselves from the habit of tensing at the moment of encounter will hit more often this way instead of bearing the lance straight where they wish to encounter, for the tensing of the body and arm at the moment of encounter makes it go off target.

Concerning how I have said that some miss by wishing always to come off best in the encounter, in my opinion every reasonable jouster should guard himself from this: you should encounter based on your assessment of yourself, the one with whom you are jousting, your horse, and your lance. And even if you know you have the advantage, you should not fear to lower your point for your opponent's shield: I don't think anyone can ever be a good jouster unless he is willing to take chances sometimes.

Apart from what I have already written, you should attend to these two counsels. First, when the lance drops underarm, if your opponent has not come very close, you should bear it a little lower than the place where you wish to encounter. This is done for two reasons: first, to have a more unobstructed view of the place where you intend to direct your lance; secondly in order not to fall lower when you track from high to low. The second counsel, in which stands the principal force of encountering well, is that you should hold your eyes firm, and focus your body and will as much as you can until it seems that you see the tines of your coronel align with the place where you want to hit.

Having written so much in counsels that pertain to jousting, I would like to write about how you should be served with footmen, even though it isn't relevant to fluidity: I have seen many people poorly served by them owing to lack of knowledge, even though they had them in abundance.

If a jouster has three footmen, in order to be better served by them with less effort, he should put two at the ends of the tilt, and one in the middle. Those at the ends should have three assignments. First, when the jouster comes, they should keep him from the tilt and make him turn in a safe place: I have seen many people injured in the feet, when tilts did not have markers at the ends, as is now the custom, trying to turn their horses before they had fully cleared the tilt, and colliding against the sides. The second is to pull the jouster's feet out of the stirrups, as required by the jouster. The third is to hold the jouster's horse in place wherever he wants it to be.

The one at the middle should have three other main assignments: first, to keep an eye on the jouster, in case he should have need in the encounter, and run to his aid quickly if it happens. Second, to collect his spear and give it to the mounted servant. Third, to watch in case any equipment falls in the encounter, and hand it over to someone who is attending the jouster.

However many footmen you have, they should always be divided into three groupings with these roles, and they will serve better and with less trouble than having them all with you in a cluster.

Chapter 11: How to encounter in the hunt

To fulfil my promise to give instructions for encountering well in the hunt, I find that generally we encounter quarry of any sort in one of four ways. First, heading toward us. Second, crossing on either side. Third, running away from us. Fourth, when the hounds have trapped it, or for some other reason it is lying still or stationary. For each of these I will write briefly the manner you should observe for encountering well and delivering a greater blow, and striking more keenly, and guarding yourself against some faults and hazards into which some people fall for lack of knowledge.

When we are jousting at a quarry, we will approach it from its front, from either side, or from behind it. If from the front, you should observe this manner: turn your horse's head aside as you come to it, making it come to the right of your horse's shoulder or flank so that it passes to the right side. For if it comes straight on, you will miss more easily, and your horse will collide on top of the quarry, and you cannot guard against it or keep the spear in your hand if you strike it well. When it comes to the encounter, you should concentrate on striking it between the shoulders, for this is where you should encounter a bear, bull, or boar from horseback, if you are riding a reasonably large mount who can manage it: it is the midpoint on the quarry, and it stands to reason that you will be less likely to miss; also, if the spear penetrates the ribcage, you can expect to hit the heart or lungs, which will kill it more easily.

When you joust at them this way, you should observe this manner for dealing them a great blow: if you are not especially strong and are not leaning forward with the spear, at the moment of encounter, squeeze the spear well in your hand, and bear down on it as you strike. Anyone who knows well how to do this, even if he is weak, will give a much greater spear-blow than someone who is considerably stronger. To do it well, you should keep these five rules in mind. First, as you arrive, turn the horse's head aside. Second, keep your eye where you have to strike, and direct your spear there. Third, bear down on it. Fourth, hold it or drop it depending on how the blow goes. Fifth, remember your spurs, to keep your horse from getting hurt.

If you are very strong, or you are leaning forward with the spear, you can omit bearing down on it, but only squeeze the spear as the tip jerks, as will happen; for between you going forward and the quarry coming toward you, you can expect that it will receive a great impact. And you should recall the other four rules, and also keep yourself firm in the saddle, for some people forget it at this moment. Even if you are going slowly, if the spear is forward, you should avoid moving your body, lest you miss by making it wander; and since its weight forces you to hold it so tight, as long as you encounter straight and the spear does not break, you can expect it to deliver a sufficiently great blow.

Some joust in a different manner with bears and boars, which is rather dangerous, and one must be very careful in it. This happens when the quarry are fleeing away from where they have offspring, and feeling themselves borne down upon they turn so suddenly that few can protect themselves from them; for they come right to the horse's face. Because this is something unexpected, one can lose control easily; and since the horse loses contact in the bit, it stumbles on top of the quarry, and is lucky to get out of it without falling.

To avoid such a hazard, you should pay heed to this as best you can: consider the nature of the place where you are going, and if you see a situation where you are worried about this kind of turn, you should rein in the horse, and veer to the side, overtaking the animal at a run on the spear-side. And when you are even with it, at once you should joust without delay, if that is what you want to do. And as you prepare to encounter, observe the aforementioned manner when it comes to the horse's shoulder. If you come across, direct the horse toward the quarry on the spear-side, so that you can strike it with the spear underarm. And when you cannot do it in any of these ways, it is better to pass quickly and turn on the quarry, directing yourself as you should, rather than to prepare to encounter from a bad position. If it comes to the left side, you should not hold the spear underarm, but take it in both hands; and do not direct your horse against it, but take the horse across and prepare to encounter in such a way that when you strike it, the quarry passes in back and not in front. This is one manner by which those who practice striking this way do it well and securely.

If you come on the quarry from behind, when you want to prepare to encounter, the best manner is to leave it to the left side, and turning in the saddle, take the spear with both hands, and so strike it. For if it comes to the right side, you can only hold the spear in one hand, and holding it this way, you cannot expect to deliver such a great blow with it. When taking the spear with both hands, sometimes people abandon the reins entirely; others take them in the right hand, holding them toward the tip of the spear; and some hold them in the left, with the spear above them. This depends on how you find best to do it.

When the quarry comes from the right side to the left, not meaning to joust,[21] but to pass, the best way is to rein in the horse and turn its head toward where the quarry is going, not rushing so much in running that the quarry ends up behind the horse's haunches, but coming even with it, making it run, and striking it from a distance. If it comes this way from the left to the right, if you have the practice of striking with both hands, observe the manner described above. If you are only accustomed to strike on the right side, and you want to give it an encounter as it comes across, urge the horse on to make the quarry pass behind the horse's haunches, turn, and work in your manner. This turn can be made at a distance or close up, depending on how nimble and responsive your mount is. If it is nimble and

---

[21] Duarte uses "joust" to refer to a head-on encounter by opponents, even if one of them is not human.

highly responsive, the closer you make it turn, the better you will strike; and if the contrary, doing it from a distance will be of greater advantage.

When the quarry is running away from you, it can be encountered well in two ways.

First, bearing the spear underarm, leaning well forward, and pursuing it well: all the force of the blow comes from the motion of the horse, directing the spear to the place where you wish to encounter, but not moving the body or arm.

The second is bearing the spear without leaning forward: when it is near, put your body into it and extend your arm to strike to your target. This way you strike more quickly and freely, but you do not deliver such great blows as with the momentum of the horse.

From such encountering often arises the hazard that, when the quarry feels itself wounded, it crosses in front of the horse's face, and often falls on it. To guard against this, you can observe one of these three ways:

First, in pursuing it and arriving from a distance to where it is going, as you strike it, turn the horse outwards, so that you do everything next to the quarry, and leaving it to the spear-side, the horse is on the other side.

The second is this: having pursued the quarry to where you can strike to the middle of its body, allow yourself to pursue it further so that you can attack it from the side or in front. This is because being struck in the forward part of its body, even if it wants to turn, the spear does not allow it, but makes it veer to the outside. If you struck to the rear part, the blow of the spear would make it turn around more readily before the horse's face.

The third way is used by some who strike a quarry with a great blow, so that it turns on the horse's face: they make the planted spear pass under the horse's neck, turning to the right side. When such a blow plants itself well, no matter how big the quarry is, it is quickly forced to the ground, if the spear is stout.

A fourth manner for striking a bear, bull, or great and heavy boar, which I consider safer than any of the aforementioned manners, provided you have a place where you can do it properly: the rider pursues the quarry well, and as you come even with it, keep it on your left side, then turn, and come across to it, passing behind to strike to its rear from your right side. When the blow prompts it to try to turn, the horse has already passed, so it is less dangerous, even though the quarries one strikes this way are all strong and formidable.

To strike more readily, my lord the king offers some recommendations in his *Book on Hunting*: not to rely on locking the spear under your arm, in order not to compromise your aim, and to let the quarry career or run along the lower slopes of the mountain, so that it does not turn.[22] I will not discuss this any further, since what he wrote pertains more to knowledge of good hunting than to the fluidity about which I am writing, so that I may finish up, having already covered three of the situations with which I began.

When a quarry is taken by the hounds, or lies still or stays in place in some other way, it is more suitable to strike overhand, but if you want to joust against it, the best way is to bear the spear without leaning forward, and deliver a blow bearing down upon it. For conducting yourself in this manner, you will strike more certainly and it will give you more fluidity to direct the horse well; if you bear the spear forward and try to strike with the momentum of the horse, you will have less control over the weapon, and it will be more dangerous for the hounds.

Chapter 12: Instructions for striking with the spear overhand

To strike well overhand, you should heed these precepts:

First you should consider whether it is against something rigid, such as armor or a thick-skinned boar, or if you are striking in a spot that is unarmored and of such a nature that the spear penetrates easily. If you are striking a strong target, firm the spear well in your hand, relax your arm, and with fluidity deliver the greatest blow you can; for that will do all the injury, and it will not help at all to bear down on it. If you are striking on something unarmored that the spear can easily penetrate, you should not trouble to lift your arm much, but squeeze the spear in your hand and hold it poised with your body, with your elbow high. When you strike, bear down on

---

[22] João I, *Livro da Montaria*, pp. 318–21, 420. João's advice against holding the spear underarm refers specifically to hunters on foot.

it and put your arm into it with the spear. This way sometimes you deliver the blow with four forces:

> First, with the motion of the horse.
> Second, with the initial striking of the arm.
> Third, with the body-weight.
> Fourth, putting your hand into it with the spear as much as you can.

If you know how to do this well, you can pass right through even a bear, bull, or boar, if you plant the blow well and choose a good spear, and do not come up against any bones that get in the way. When you strike this way, you should intend to pass right through from one side to the other; for if you intend only to strike, once the spear hits the surface, you go no further, while if you try to pass right through, and accustom yourself to doing this, your body and arm continue to bear down on the spear until it passes no further. Those who are good riders, very fluid and sure, do it with such despatch that others who see it, if they don't have good knowledge of it, would take it for a single blow. And this is a general rule for striking overhand.

For further explanation, those who hunt big game can do so three ways: with the quarry coming toward them, fleeing them, or with hounds holding them. When you come at the joust, the best way is to hold your hand still near your face, with your elbow high, and prepare to encounter so that it collides onto the spear as if you had it underarm; as it hits the target, put your strength behind it wherever it strikes, bearing down on it. This way you plant the weapon better and deliver a much greater spear-blow, if it is something the spear can penetrate. Those who lift their arm often miss, with the quarry passing before they can strike.

If it is running away as you come to it, to strike it more readily, you should not wait until you catch right up with it, but before you get there put your body and arm forward. It often happens that in striking this way the animal comes to you and turns to bear down onto the spear, and you can deliver great blows this way. This manner of striking gives rise to a hazard, for as the quarry does this, feeling that it has been struck, it turns between the horse's forefeet, and since your body is forward, it is hard to keep from falling, for the forward force without help of the reins throws you. And to give a bigger and more certain blow, it is best not to hasten until you have caught right up with it, and strike bearing downward on the spear, not putting the body forward.

If the hounds have the quarry, the blow should be delivered with your arm held close in to you, and not lifting it much, and keeping the horse reined in, targeting from a distance; do not stop the horse at the moment of striking, but urge it quickly forward, and as you arrive turn it aside, and immediately strike where you mean to, without inhibition of will. For if you stop and strike standing still, you will always deliver a smaller and slower blow. Those who know how to do it well can strike quite safely in the presence of two or three dogs without being slowed down, displaying great fluidity through such mastery; even if the horse passes by, provided you keep the horse reined in, you can bear down with your body and arm to give a great spear-blow.

To bring any quarry to the ground, I have found a particular technique if you have a spear with a strong shaft and a well secured head: in striking, if I enter well and pull it across with a jolt, bearing down toward the ground, it works like a lever, so that few animals can keep from falling, especially if I do it with the motion of the horse. But many spears get broken this way.

When a dog gets the boar, you should take this advice: see whether the boar continues along with the dog, or turns. If it goes straight, it is good to run as fast as you can, and strike it; if it turns around, it is better to run more reined in. With any of these ways, in order to hunt well and display good fluidity, it is better to strike in passing than after you stop.

From these precepts on how to strike in hunting you can derive instruction how to deliver greater, more accurate, and speedier spear-blows in battle. And it seems to me a very good custom in hunting to bear big and heavy spears, for if you master the art with these, you will find the light ones much easier. I have found this through my own experience, for no riders carry bigger and heavier spears than in my household. As to the practice of those who carry them light, it offers no advantage in striking well and speedily in the hunt. And I boast of this to give a concrete example and because I am experienced in hunting: in this case one can certainly boast without blame, as long as one does so with reason and truth.

Chapter 13: How to throw a spear

Four things are necessary for someone who wants to throw the spear well:

> First, to throw far.
> Second, accurately.
> Third, safely, keeping himself and his horse from falling.
> Fourth, elegantly.

As to the first, whoever wants to do it well should practice first on foot, throwing spears that would be reasonable to use on horseback: it is natural for people to learn throwing this way, and you cannot hope to throw well from horseback something you have not first learned to throw on foot.

In throwing on foot, some people bear the spear low as they run, and others high, and throw it from there. The former seems to me the better way for throwing on horseback. But I could not do it this way: I bear it high, and when I am ready to throw, lower the arm and body, and send it up without delay. Both of these seem just fine to me. But to extend the arm early in the beginning of the run, or after you lower it to tarry with it there, does not seem good to me.

To deliver a great throw from horseback, you should start by teaching yourself with a spear shaft blunted on both ends for safety. Bringing the horse to the canter, work to relax your arm as if you were throwing on foot, and release it high and smoothly, having squeezed it in your hand, well aimed for distance; for when the spear is released this way, the motion of the horse makes it travel much further than you might think. You should practice this way at the canter for a while, so that you can better get all these precepts, especially the fling of the arm, for few do it well enough. And among other things you should know how to recognize the forward balance you should give the spear to make it go smoothly, and as you run, squeeze on it so that, when you throw it, the point goes straight where you want it to go. Once you have been able to do this for a few days at the canter using such a shaft, you can practice with any other projectiles on horseback, always practicing to throw a spear more than anything else.

On foot, avoid using a bar or other heavy projectile, nor very light, which can wrench your arm;[23] throwing a spear on horseback should never cause pain, if your arm is not already injured. The benefit of these two kinds of throwing is minimal for someone who is a good thrower on horseback, and the displeasure that one feels in losing it is pretty great, as I have experienced myself.

If you want to make a long throw, you should have a horse with a jennet saddle with short stirrups, as is customary, and it should run well and have a somewhat hard mouth; you should use a spear that is appropriately sized for you, keeping your arm fluid and limber. Run on a flat course with your back to the wind, and when you reach the first houses of the city,[24] fling the spear with your arm, not tightening on the bit at all except after throwing, and observing the other precepts that I offered at the beginning.

This way you should throw about a third further than on foot. I have tested this, having made a throw that exceeded 16 spear-lengths; when I dismounted and ran on foot in the same place, dressed only in my jupon with the same spear, I could reach little more than 11. I offer this example here for everyone to recognize whether he has reached his potential in this art, realizing the advantage that he can get with his spear on horseback compared to when he throws on foot.

When you want to throw, you should also do your best to avoid all the contraries of the aforementioned advantages that you should ensure to make great throws. And because the baulking of the horse at the moment of throwing is a major impediment, to make sure you avoid this, once you start the run, you should not apply the spurs heavily before you throw, but let him run as he wants, and just before you throw, give him the spurs hard again, and as his gait picks up, promptly throw with the least possible delay.

---

[23] The iron bar was one of the projectiles used in throwing contests; light projectiles included the small throwing stone known in Spanish as the *volandera* (Monte 1492: sig. z4v; Monte 1509: sig. a4v).

[24] the first houses of the city: *algum começo de cidade*. The meaning here is unclear, but may refer to the practice of these sports on broad streets that also served as entry-points to towns. I am indebted to Rita Costa Gomes for this interpretation.

To throw accurately, you should consider whether the throw is short or long. If it is long, help yourself with your skill at throwing and throw it as far in advance as you estimate the quarry can go before the spear arrives; this throw will have a chance of hitting. If it is short, you should not throw straight ahead, since that is dangerous and not so accurate, but let it go it to whichever side suits you or the situation; affix your gaze on the shoulder of the quarry, and aim it there, throwing high and easily, as if you were playing at the javelin,[25] not making such great account of trying to deliver a powerful throw as of planting it. For if the spear goes smoothly from the hand, the motion of the horse usually makes it deliver a great enough blow. If you throw standing still, as often happens for hunters, and it is reasonably close, you should observe the same manner of throwing high and easily as if you were playing at the javelin, a game I have found very good for a man to train himself to throw accurately on foot and on horseback.

To throw safely, you need only observe two things. First, you should never throw straight in front of you. Second, you should practice that as the spear leaves your hand, you turn your horse in the opposite direction from where you are throwing.

To do it elegantly, you should heed three things. First, you must have a suitable horse, saddle, outfit, and spear. Second, you should keep your feet, legs, and body still, and principally throw with your arm; and you should not unsteady yourself from the saddle when you throw. Third, observing the aforementioned precepts, you should deliver a powerful and smooth throw with the spear.

Heavy spears call for keeping the shoulder and the entire arm fluid, and light ones and canes chiefly from the middle of the arm. In throwing I have struck many bears, boars, and harts from horseback, while at times I missed others owing to the horse, saddle, or wind, the ground where I was running, a dry or cold hand, obstruction of the arm, weight, a bad spear, or haste of will; but I never considered it strange when I missed, since these factors and other occurrences can get in the way. And even though people do not use this art much when their arms are armored, this is no reason not to practice and know it, for at some time it may be of use. And I have often been successful and displayed

---

[25] javelin: Port. *dardo*. See the Introduction on throwing sports.

good fluidity in hunting and cane-games and other things that good men are accustomed to do on horseback and on foot.

Chapter 14: How to strike with a sword

As to teaching how to strike well with a sword, it seems to me that logically one can strike on horseback in four ways:

> First, with a horizontal forehand cut [*talho travesso*].
> Second, with a backhand cut [*revés*].
> Third, with a vertical cut [*fendente*] from high to low.
> Fourth, with a thrust [*ponta*].

I consider the first and second best for striking an opponent on horseback. To deliver a great blow forehand, you should strike with the motion of the horse and body and with the flow of the arm all together. I have found this very suitable in tourneying; for if I strike standing still, just with the arm, I deliver a rather weak blow, but with the motion of the horse and the flow of the body and the arm combined, the blow will be considerably greater.

And here is a rule for anyone who wants to deliver fine blows in a tourney: you should normally strike while in motion, firming yourself on your legs, relaxing your body and arm, squeezing the sword well in your hand; and do not deliver the blow straight across or vertically, but obliquely downwards. And for this you should not make tight turns in a grand tourney, nor focus your attention on one opponent, unless to get such advantage against him from behind or the side as will please you in order to display your great mastery.

If you are riding a good horse who is responsive to the spurs, bold, and well trained, at the first clash get each of your targets, and stay reined in to avoid an unexpected fall, as happens to many at such times. And after you first meet an opponent, always strike in a specific place, and once you deliver to one, afterwards go to another without worrying about turning around until you have passed the entire field, seeking the most visible places on the field. And where you see some of your teammates standing close to the opponents, striking hard among them, scatter them with the impetus of the horse, pass quickly and go to strike someone else. This way you obtain these advantages:

First, you are highly visible, because you seek in every direction.

Second, you give greater strokes, because you strike whomever it suits you; and you will find many who are well placed for you to strike at will without any obstruction.

Third, you and your horse work more easily, for you do not have to tire it with running or turning, but generally bring it to a canter when you wish to make a particular arrival.

Also, since you deliver your blows at intervals, your arm does not get tired. The reverse will happen if you tourney with just a single opponent: if you go back and forth on your horse to strike, each time the opponent must gain an advantage, for it makes work for both you and your horse; and if you strike standing still, your arm soon becomes tired, and the small intervals between the blows make them appear rather weak to the onlookers. Therefore personal experience tells me that whoever wishes to have the advantages in tourneying that I have described should observe the aforementioned manner.

To strike with a reverse, you should do it solely with the flow of the arm, and likewise in battle when necessary.

The cut from high to low can rarely deliver a great blow to someone else on horseback. With men on foot or game animals, whom you can strike this way, you should never pull with the sword, which will make it cut less, and easily strike your foot or horse, but bear downwards on the blow with all your body, squeezing the sword well in your hand; this way you will deliver a much greater blow, other things being equal with the sword and the thing you are striking.

As I have said, practice is the principal basis for learning all arts and, once they are learned, for keeping them from being forgotten. Anyone who wants to possess this art should continually practice cutting with the sword on horseback and on foot, bearing it well, because he will receive such advantage from it that his desire will increase to do it more, and the practice will give him advantage in the art. And I advise anyone who wants to have a good arm for this, and for throwing a spear, not to play tennis in a wide place,[26] or play

---

[26] Tennis courts were not standardized in the late Middle Ages; the game was normally played in a walled space comparable to a modern squash court, in a

throwing sports with very heavy or very light projectiles; for a good arm can easily be ruined in these arts of little worth.

Striking with a thrust calls for the manner described above for the spear used overhand, striking with the arm and bearing down behind it. And you can strike a quarry at a distance straight in front of yourself, and on the outside, in order to keep it from making a turn into the horse's face when it feels itself injured. The safest is to strike it with a thrust on the outside going across.

I have written rather comprehensively about these arts for the reasons I have already laid out concerning the profit that it can bring to some, and because it seems to me that they are a great foundation for good horsemen to display their fluidity. And because the practice of various places and times alters arts and customs, perhaps some readers will believe the opposite of what I am writing. Therefore you should know that I write on the basis of my own experience, which agrees with the most general good practice used at present in the territories of the king, my lord and father, may God keep his soul. I do not say this to boast (even though concerning these minor arts a man can freely say what he believes to be true), but I do it to cite the authority of my writing, so that whoever reads this will know that I am not writing based on what I have heard, but based on what I have learned through extensive practice.

And I offer one more bit of advice to lords on the subject of fluidity and the benefit that it can bring to them: you should sometimes practice mounting from the ground without any aid on the saddle, and without anyone else holding the horse by the reins or by either of the stirrups. You should practice this from both the right and left sides, sometimes holding a spear in hand, and at others a hunting bird over your right foot;[27] and you should even do it in full armor. It also seems to me a good exercise to remount from one horse to another on both sides; and it is better to go from the smaller to the

---

version that survives as "real tennis" today. Related ball games were sometimes played in open areas, and some of these might fall within Duarte's definition of "tennis" (*jogo de peella*). The implication here may be that the wider the playing area, the greater the strain on the player's arm. See Gillmeister, *Tennis: A Cultural History*, pp. 35–83; John McClelland, "Ball games", pp. 52–53.

[27] hunting bird: *aves pera caçar* (see above p. 49 fn. 5). Hunting birds are normally held in the left hand; "right" may be an error here.

larger, or if they are of equal size, then to position the one you are mounting on higher ground, or to grab onto someone standing on foot between them.

For it is written in the book *On the Governance of Princes* that when Roman knights were not at war, they had wooden horses set up in their houses, which they saddled and practiced mounting in armor from both sides, recognizing how beneficial this art is.[28] You should also practice vaulting over the saddle in your normal clothing, if it is not too encumbering, even if the horse is large; for if we practice it, we will do it reasonably well, as long as we are not naturally heavy. I have found this by experience, for when I was practicing this, I never found a horse so tall that I could not vault over it with ease, even in full clothing. And when I ceased to practice it, I found myself much diminished as a result. Moreover a lord's status is no impediment to practicing this, for even if in public places they are no longer bothering to pay attention to their reins and stirrups, preferring to preen themselves, in hunting and hawking and in traveling they should turn to this practice, and they will certainly find great advantage in it.

I have seen a good example of this in my lord the king, to whom God grant glory: having practiced this when he was young, by the time he had passed seventy years,[29] he could mount a horse of reasonable height from the ground without other aid more easily than most tall men of fifty. Based on the good and bad things that I have seen in him and others, and on my opinions based on experience of such practice, I have written this advice about things pertaining to fluidity, which I believe you will find profitable if you choose to practice it.

---

[28] Duarte is referring to the thirteenth-century *De Regimine Principum* by Giles of Rome (Aegidius Romanus), Bk. 3 pt. 3 ch. 7: "Vegetius tells us that the ancients fashioned wooden horses, on which youths would exercise indoors in the winter, and outdoors in the summer; at first they would mount the horses without armor, and afterwards with it; this way they learned to mount those horses from the left and right and from every direction." The inventory of Duarte's library indicates that he owned two copies of this book; see Duarte, *Livro dos conselhos*, pp. 206–7. On Vegetius, see below, p. 138 fn. 30.

[29] João was born in 1358, so Duarte is here referring to the period after 1428.

Chapter 15: In praise of the arts

I have written at some length about these arts that people practice on horseback on account of the custom and great affection that I have had for them, and likewise of the other arts of strength, agility, and skill at throwing that knights and squires in this land have known and practiced most excellently. These days I find this to be lacking—something I find most displeasing—in spite of the words and counsels I have offered, with some measure of teaching and instruction about it. At other times, compelled by order to practice them, people do them in a manner that seems to offer little enjoyment in comparison to what I have seen in my household. I believe this arises from lack of will that they have toward these arts. For they prefer chatting with women, and their desire is entirely focused on wearing fine clothing and shoes, playing tennis, singing, and dancing, conforming to the wills of women, who are mainly interested in these arts, so that they largely abandon all the others. And because the principal cause is affection of will, in its absence they neither know nor wish to learn these arts, and the things they once knew quickly fall into oblivion. I truly think this reflects the vicissitudes of the world, which grants these arts in each land and realm at various times to whomever it pleases—its basis is not easy to comprehend.

I have seen even more in my household: as long as I practiced these arts, both those which are followed today and also those which are abandoned, high-ranking people who lived with me did similarly, and others took example from them. When I ceased to practice them owing to great preoccupations, so did the great ones, and likewise most of the lesser ones, who always follow the leaders in the household, taking into account ages, offices, and manners of living. For young knights and squires in the household look to the great lords as models for how to conduct themselves and practice arts: when the leaders praise and practice arts, the majority pursue them. If great lords do not undertake or wish to practice them, I do not expect lesser people to get such practice of them as will be of great use.

Every household or kingdom takes great example in such things from the example of lords and princes, as I have said. It is the same with the pursuit of virtues, in which today I see good outcomes, thanks be to God: through the great goodness and virtue that were always present in the king my lord and father, most victorious and of great virtues, and in the very virtuous queen, my lady and mother, the principal men of their household and all the others of the realm, by grace that was granted to them, made great strides in abandoning evil customs and increasing in virtues. So while I criticize my countrymen for the decline of good physical arts, I believe that at present we are worthy to be praised for the practice of virtues and abandonment of evils and iniquities, thanks be to God.

Yet the practice of virtues should not eliminate the practice of good physical arts that have always been praised and commended by lords and great men, as we can well see in the book by Vegetius, *De Re Militari*, and in other books of history and instruction about the deeds of war.[30] Even though those arts currently practiced may be good, our role in society is that of defenders, and so the principal arts we should learn and possess are the ones most suitable to the needs of battle. Therefore I advise lords and other gentle folk to whom these arts pertain, to consider that their bodies are just like their estates: if they are not well cultivated, they will naturally yield thorns and thistles and other plants of little worth; and by working and tilling and improving them, they produce the fruits from which we have our main sustenance in this life. If in youth our bodies are left idle,

---

[30] Publius Flavius Vegetius Renatus was a Roman military strategist and author of the enormously influential *De Re Militari*, also known as *Epitoma Rei Militaris*, composed sometime between 383 and 450. For an English translation, see *Vegetius: Epitome of Military Science*, transl. Milner. Piel (p. 119, n. 1) conjectures that Duarte did not know the text directly but through John of Salisbury's *Policraticus* (circa 1159). Duarte's most likely second-hand source, however, is Giles of Rome's *De Regimine Principum*, whom he elsewhere cites as a source for information from Vegetius (see above, p. 131 fn. 28). But recent research on the diffusion and impact of Vegetius in Portugal presents compelling evidence that Duarte did in fact know the text first-hand. Sir Peter Russell pieces together archival evidence that the Infante Pedro, Duke of Coimbra composed a now-lost Portuguese translation of Vegetius in the 1430s, dedicated to Duarte. João Gouveia Monteiro and Christopher Allmand have likewise argued persuasively that late medieval Portuguese military tacticians, including Duarte, were influenced by Vegetius to an extent that suggests first-hand knowledge. See Russell, 'Terá havido uma tradução medieval portuguesa do *Epitome rei militaris* de Vegécio?', Monteiro, *A guerra em Portugal nos finais da Idade Media*, vol. I, pp. 267–82, and Allmand, *The 'De re militari' of Vegetius*, p. 175.

because we fail to apply ourselves to good sciences or good arts or physical activities, according as pertains to each person, they turn out so useless that they ought to become the property of others, who can make them serve as serfs and do some profitable thing according to their state and disposition, rather than idly consume the provisions that are eagerly desired, increased, and managed by good workers.

To expunge such error, children of good lineage who are raised in such households as are capable of it, should be taught at a young age to read, write, and speak Latin, spending time with good books in Latin and the vernacular about good conduct in a virtuous life. Some people say that such reading is not especially suitable for men of high estate, but I believe that since we must all believe that we have souls, we should above all work with the grace of the Lord for their salvation, which is greatly facilitated (with His grace) by the study of good books and good discourse. Likewise people should study books of moral philosophy, which are of many kinds for teaching good customs and pursuit of virtues, and they should practice well all the things pertaining to it. Books teaching about warfare, such as the venerable chronicles, are very pertinent reading for lords and knights and their sons: from them we can derive excellent examples and knowledge that are of great assistance in times of need, with the grace of God.

The good physical arts that pertain to everybody according to their estate should never be neglected, particularly riding and wrestling, which are the foundation from which one proceeds to the greatest honors: good riding brings great help in all the arts that are practiced on horseback, and wrestling makes us lose fear in those which are practiced on foot. It also greatly fosters overall strength of body and good constitution, which greatly helps in military actions and all good arts. If we were not well trained and taught in youth, we can reasonably acquire these arts as adults. Gentlemen who know and practice these arts in noble households make the members of the household more cheerful, free of irritability, of greater fame and more feared, as long as they have a reasonable share of other virtues and good qualities as befits them. And thanks to these arts they will be more valued by their lords, and receive more favor than their peers who do nothing special in their service, or fail to display any art that will foster a good opinion of them or do honor to their lord's household, or provide enjoyment and good entertainment for their lord's servants and others who come to him, unlike people who do practice them well.

Chapter 16: A brief description of wrestling techniques[31]

For the reasons I have just mentioned, I have had a summary of wrestling techniques written up. If someone wants to know more about them, he should ask some good master of this art to teach them, for this material is written more as an aide-memoire than with the expectation that anyone can learn these techniques from what I have written.

These are the ones that I have generally used and seen practiced by good wrestlers—not all of them by any one person, but based on each individual's custom and style.

The *travessa encambada*[32] is delivered in two places: one at the arm, the other behind the neck, placing the head under the arm.

The other *travessa* is delivered in five ways: one at the arm; another, the "forsaken" [*desemparada*], disengaging suddenly, and at once delivering it at the neck; the other delivering the *alça-perna* or the *cambadella* at the neck, and suddenly turning across; and the other reverse *travessa*, grasping by one arm and turning to deliver it over the other; in another manner, when someone delivers the arm to the neck, grasping the arm thus suddenly, and delivering it.

Item, the *alça-perna*[33] is delivered underarm, and at the neck, and at the arm.

---

[31] As Duarte tells us, this chapter is not meant to be intelligible to someone who is not already familiar with the techniques. Although these may be known to modern martial artists, most are not identifiable from their medieval Portuguese names, and the translation here does not try to impose clarity on them. Any attempt to make sense of this material will need to rely heavily on Pietro Monte, who shares much of Duarte's vocabulary but offers considerably more explanatory specifics (Monte 1492: sig. x3r–y6r; Monte 1509: sig. a1r–a3r, c4r–c7v).

[32] The *travessa* ("traverse") may be the same as Monte's *torno*, a rotational leg-throw, which Monte also calls the *traversa*.

[33] Lit. "lift-leg"; probably the same as Monte's *ancha*, a hip-throw, which he also calls the *tolle-perna*, meaning the same thing in Latin as Duarte's Portuguese term.

Item, the *cambadella* is delivered in all three of these places; the difference is that the *alça-perna* throws forward, and the *cambadella* backward. One can also deliver the *cambadella* behind the neck, like the *travessa encambada*.

Item, the *sacalinha*[34] is delivered in three ways: by the heel, the toe, and reversed.

Item, the straight *desvio*,[35] in six ways: one from the arms, not embracing; the next embracing; lifting on high, and then delivering the *desvio*; the next also embracing, and deflecting him to one side, and turning him to deliver to the other; and the *desvio* of the body; and the other at the neck.

The reverse *desvio* in three ways: one bowed arm to bowed arm,[36] embracing, and thus deliver it; the next only from the arms and legs, without embracing; and the last from the neck.

Item, the *lombo*,[37] which some deliver standing up, others with the knee on the ground; and it is always delivered at the arm.

Item, the *quadril* is delivered at the bowed arm, and sometimes at the arm, and others reversed in the manner of the reverse *travessa*.

Item, the *persaida* is delivered grabbing either arm from outside, and so deliver to the leg on that side while withdrawing backward.

Item, the *mamillo*, which is delivered grabbing by the neck from one side, and deliver it with the foot from the other side in the manner of the *desvio*, but throw backwards.

Item, the "technique of the dog" [*erro do cam*]: grab bowed arm to bowed arm, and deliver the foot past either leg, and throw him backwards, making an effort to squeeze with the arms and load the body.

Item, the *tavascom* is delivered pressing with the arm across the chest, and delivering the foot against the other side.

Item, the *bico*: place the foot at the ankle on either leg, and press with the body, and thus step forward with one foot to throw him.

---

[34] Monte's *sacaliña* is a leg-hook that throws the opponent backwards.

[35] In Monte, the *desvio* is a kind of hip-throw.

[36] bowed arm: *arca*. The term can also refer to the chest, but Vieyra (*Dictionary*, sv. arca) gives this as a technical alternative in wrestling. The technique described below under "grasping of the bowed arms" makes more sense if Duarte means the arm rather than the chest.

[37] Possibly related to Monte's *deslomada*, a technique executed against the opponent's lower back.

Item, grasping of the bowed arms is done in two ways: one suddenly making it seem that you mean to grasp him by the neck, and when he lifts his arms, grasp him by them; the other entering bowed arm to bowed arm and unbalance him, and put the other arm on the other bowed arm, not releasing the one you already have.

Item, the *trazeiras* can be taken in three manners: one grasping the hand, and unbalance him, and leap back; the other embracing to either arm, and lowering deflect him with the body and leap back, not letting go of that arm; and the last when you seek to grasp by the neck, sliding the *trazeiras*.

The ways to throw backward are generally three: first, lifting in the arms, and throw on either side; second, going around until he has a moment of heedlessness, and from there loosen with the arms or deflect him by the feet or throw; third, deliver the foot past the opponent's leg as in the "technique of the dog", and throw forward.

Item, to throw by the bowed arm, lift and throw to either side, or deliver the "technique of the dog" with one foot; and if you cannot lift with the one, at once try with the other.

Item, the neck: when he grasps, make him let go by unbalancing the shoulders and crossing the hand or arm on the opponent's throat, and throw him across suddenly, and grasp either of his arms.

Item, it is a good technique little practiced, when grasping someone with one arm by the neck, squeeze if he lowers himself, as most people will, jump to the outside, and hold him hard by the neck, bearing down on him with your body, and make him come to the ground on his knees.

Item, since many people in other countries, when they wrestle in clothing, have the practice of locking us up by the clothes at the level of the shoulders, and impeding both arms, it is a very good technique with this to give a turn with the arm above his, deviating the body out to the side and, bearing down onto him, turning him to grasp by the bowed arm under that arm.

Or if you want to do a rather dangerous but effective play, turn the arm as I have said of the elbow against the opponent's hand, and grasp from below with the other hand to his middle, or the arm, and deviating your body, bear down with your elbow and your entire arm onto his hand; this will give him such pain that few can avoid going to their knees on the ground. But with such a technique you can break his arm or dislocate his hand, if he is not very tough or mindful, so it should not be done in friendly wrestling.

You should not suppose that this is not an art for great lords, because my lord the king, may God have his soul, used it very well; and the princes, captains, and good men-at-arms around him were so outstanding in it that one could find few of any station who were their equals. In my own court, when I praised and practiced it, there were such good wrestlers that I did not believe one could find their equals in the household of any other prince. Today it is not used the same way, but I hold this for a great failing: it would greatly please me to see a return to that good state of affairs. But it seems to me that for certain known impediments and other unfortunate circumstances, one cannot make it happen; but since there is nothing new under heaven, and things that once have been eventually return, may it please our Lord that even yet in my time we may correct this, as it once was when we practiced these things well in these realms.

Beyond these there are other special techniques that some people execute, by which they often throw; each has their deflections, blocks, circumventions, and counters, and against the deflections some manner of tripling, all of which one can learn through the will to possess this art well and through great practice. And I have written this so that readers can have occasion to ask about each technique, and because some people can learn more quickly and better than if they did not see them written up this way.

And I command you to include this chapter in this *Book on Horsemanship*, which teaches about these other arts that are carried out on horseback, even though it seems out of place in such a book: I included it on account of the great affection and good practice I have had for this art, which I see so forgotten among people of estate and good lineage, and which I greatly fear may fall into oblivion. Therefore, seeing what I have written here, remember that this art is one of the principal ones that good men should possess, and that knights and common people in these realms have possessed most excellently. For it gives them these advantages that are very helpful in actions of war:

> First, great increase in agility, which is a great advantage in all works.

Second, great improvement of strength in hands, arms, legs, and the rest of the body.

Third, fluidity, confidence, and daring to grapple with any man, however mighty he may be.

Fourth, great mastery in knowing how to grapple with our hands, and defend and sustain, according to the nature of the one with whom we come arm-to-arm.

Fifth, knowing how to deliver techniques of the feet and body, and deflect them, block them and circumvent them, according to each technique, being instantly ready at the moment of execution; for with good knowledge and great practice, the entire body will know what it needs to do in each moment of such need.

Sixth, with good knowledge and practice of this art we lose much of the reluctance and impediment to try and learn many others, because it makes the body more adept, and the others will be less difficult and less dangerous on account of this one.

Seventh, to be more praised by our lords and friends, more recognized by strangers, and more feared by our opponents, according as each of us naturally possesses the other good dispositions and advantages.

And recognizing all this in ourselves, we gain courage beyond what we have by nature, and it makes us hold ourselves in better regard, with good contentment, when we feel we have advantage in this art, in accordance with our knowledge, estate, and disposition.

Therefore I advise anyone who is of knightly rank, and others to whom it is suitable, that they should work to know this art well, and to practice it well according as is suitable for them; for although it will never entirely vanish in those who know it well and have resolute wills, as long as strength does not greatly fail them, the lack of reasonable practice brings great decline in this and all other arts.

This is the end of Section 5 and the beginning of Section 6, teaching how to strike with the spurs and how they should be, and how you should sometimes govern a horse with a stick or rod

[Chapter 1: How to strike with the spurs]

Reason and will urge us to bring to completion that which we begin well, as long as we are not prevented by legitimate impediments; and so, God willing, I will continue this text in which I have written little for the past four years,[38] with the intention I wrote of in the beginning, finishing it off more briefly. For the great cares that increased for me since (by the grace of God) I was made king have allowed me little time to work on it: I get no opportunities save those I can find amidst the interference from the other great matters by which I am burdened, as I wrote in the beginning.

Adhering to my initial plan, in this short chapter I will offer some instruction on how to strike with the spurs, the styles of spurs, and how mounts should sometimes be governed with a rod or stick; and explaining the errors, I will show the good manner that you should observe in it, with additional special precepts that are profitable for particular situations.

In striking with the spurs people err by excess, omission, or not observing the situation or reasonable manner. Some people err by excess, if the mount goes slowly, owing to limited knowledge and bad habits: they repeatedly goad it, making it recalcitrant. If the horse is naturally lazy and reluctant, this practice increases the problem, for things much used make less feeling. This same issue arises in running: if the horse tends to baulk, constant application of the spurs will make it increase greatly in this habit; if it is frisky, such a practice will make it more so. In doing a great run, there is nothing that causes greater impediment than excessive striking with the spurs, for if a horse is sufficient for running a league in a reasonable manner when it is temperately struck, excessive spurring will make it lose speed within a single bowshot. In addition, excessive and

---

[38] Duarte is presumably referring to the years after his accession in 1433, suggesting that he resumed writing around 1437.

inappropriate striking with the spurs will make it less responsive to direction, and become badly bitted and "give to the seat".[39] All these evils come to the mount from excessive use of the spurs, leading to displeasure, danger, obstruction, exhaustion, and bad appearance in all the principal things by which good riders are recognized, which come from good striking with the spurs as required in every situation. Therefore, when you do more than you should, good riders judge it for a fault, and it makes you look bad: steadiness is one of the things that looks good on horseback, as I have written, and excessive striking with the spurs makes the rider unsteady, taking away a large part of his good appearance.

Some riders err by omission owing to fear of the mount, as we can see in those who are afraid to give it the spurs when they should. Others do the same by excess of will, through their desire to strike: something happens to them, so in fear they hastily shake their legs to get away, and fail to make contact with the spurs. By these examples we can recognize how people fail through omission in these cases and other similar ones.

As to specific situations, I cannot list everything in which riders err by not observing good practices, so I will set forth these examples in the following arts, so that by recognizing them you can extrapolate to others.

First, when some riders joust, the moment they begin the course, they strike the horse with the spurs, and so apply them for the entire course, if they are accustomed to run hard, or the horse does not go well; and the moment before they arrive at the encounter, they cease to strike it. And because the horse fears the arrival of the opponent when it is near, and because it no longer feels the spurs, it baulks or turns aside. The opposite happens if, as the horse enters into its course, you do not give it the spurs, and just before you arrive at the encounter, you strike reasonably hard depending on what the mount requires; this way, if its will is not already fearful, it will run the course straight.

---

[39] The context suggests that being "badly bitted" and "giving to the seat" both describe unresponsiveness on the part of the horse, perhaps refusing to acknowledge signals from the bit and the rider's body respectively.

The second is in playing at cane-games or throwing some other thing, for here again some riders spur their mounts excessively at the beginning, and when they throw, they make such a show of correcting themselves, ceasing to strike them, that soon they make them baulk. They should use the spurs little in the beginning, and continue this way prior to throwing, then apply them hard, and at once throw promptly without delay.

The third concerns those who go hunting and are accustomed to strike with the spear under their arm. When they are near, because they are focused on the impending arrival, they forget the spurs, if they have little practice with them in this art. Therefore it is necessary to be more mindful of them at the moment of arrival than before, to make the horse arrive without fear.

The fourth is in making easy jumps, which calls for this manner: as the horse comes toward the jump, leave it to come at its pleasure, and just before it arrives, give it hard with the spurs, and hold yourself in the saddle without additional tightening, such that it does not fear or baulk.

The fifth is to pass in public when people are watching: so that the mount does it with a good will, let it come without striking with the spurs, and before it arrives, give it the spurs hard anew, and so it will pass better than in any other way.[40]

It is also a fault to strike hard with mounts that are very lively, and lazy ones, or not to know to give it the spurs when you should. To strike harder, it is a great advantage to bear your feet well firmed in the stirrups; riders who bear their feet poorly in the stirrups do not generally have the ability to give their mount the spurs. Therefore, in addition to the other benefits, for this reason it is very useful to hold the feet firm.

By the precepts written here you can see how you should observe the situation in striking with the spurs, and that everyone should consider what he should do, and consult with people who know how to spur the horse properly. For without doubt this is one of

---

[40] This may be a very early reference to what would become the *haute école* parade gait known as the passage or Spanish trot, a high-stepping, collected slow trot (Pluvinel, *Maneige Royal*, p. xvii and fig. 39; Liedtke, *Royal Horse and Rider*, pp. 62, 239).

the essential properties of a good rider, to know how to observe the situation and reasonable manner in striking with them, as can be seen in Sicilian horses, who wheel themselves around with their aid. Therefore anyone who wants to be a good rider should know when we should aid ourselves with them.

In the manner of striking there are errors in agitating the body or legs, opening them, angling the feet, striking too close or far from the girths, striking inconsistently, holding or bearing down on the strike, giving correction excessively, or for a long duration. Therefore, guarding against these faults, you can observe good manner in this way: your body should not move, nor the legs, except from the knees down, not opening them more than you normally have them. From there, strike with your feet straight along the mount, neither very near nor far from the girths, always in a consistent place, and whenever you apply the spurs, at once lightly lift your feet back to their place; for delaying makes the horse shake its head and baulk. Nor should you strike with them very often, but for a moderate duration as you will see good riders do; for it is not good to apply them beyond measure.

I write this speaking generally according to my custom, for I know that some Moors, owing to riding very short, bear the heels high and strike with the feet across, and often more than we do; and the Irish, not using stirrups, do not observe our practices in striking with the spurs.[41] So each nation has its way, with which I will not trouble myself, for I write chiefly to instruct my own subjects, among whom what I am setting forth seems the most approved manner.

Chapter [2]: The various types of spurs, and how to control the mount using sometimes a rod or a stick

There are many different styles of spurs: I have seen people wear them straight of moderate size; short, curving downwards; very long and some curving upwards; some with a wheel, others with a cylinder. All this seems to me to serve for various purposes: the straight ones of moderate length, for saddles that are called French, are generally good for all mounts and times; those with a cylinder

---

[41] On Irish riding, see Introduction.

and those with wheels (which according to our custom are considered more elegant and safer for the mounts) are helpful not to strike them as hard, although it bothers the horse more if they have long spikes. The downward-turning ones are good for wilful horses, so that the legs can enclose them better, and the horse does not feel it so much. Long ones are worn with leg-armor, and for some people who cannot or do not know how to strike well with others. The upturned ones allow you to spur with less effort for small mounts who require a lot.

Owing to little knowledge and understanding, some people wear them without considering the situation or reason, wearing the very long and upturned ones on both good horses and wilful ones, which is entirely backwards. Therefore anyone who can, should consider the situation, the nature of his legs, and what the mount is like. And if he has no more than a single pair, he should wear straight ones of moderate length, but with short and small spikes, for these are generally best for all times and any kind of mount.

Jennet spurs are good short, and with a small, thick spike. All spurs, of whatever fashion, should have strong irons, fittings, and leathers, so that our feet are placed just right and the buckle sits in its place for good appearance and use; for you will need their help when you least expect it, and if they are weak, they will fail, and their failure will bring even greater failings. Therefore they should be good, well made, and strong, and of a fashion that you feel is suitable for the mount you are riding, the nature of your legs, and what you have to do.

You should not care much about the changing of customs. In things that serve no other purpose but good appearance, I recommend observing the general opinion in accordance with everyone's age and estate. But where you must consider avoidance of harm, and good knowledge of beneficial arts, you should observe custom only as far as it does not mean doing something harmful and dangerous. I see this today in using immoderately long spurs: good horses cannot ride well with them, and in hunting, when people dismount hastily to run on foot, the spurs break and are ruined in such a way that it is a great scorn to see for anyone who has good knowledge of it. Therefore you should reject such custom and wear spurs of moderate design, as I have said.

One instructs, aids, and runs horses with the stick and rod at various times, regarding which I will offer some examples from which we can derive counsel and instruction that will be of benefit in similar cases.

First, in training mounts at the outset, people give their instructions with light whips. This is done so that the spurs will not give them the habit of baulking, recoiling, sucking back,[42] or not running straight; if we use spurs, new mounts often show one of these faults. They use whips before sticks, to make the horse fear correction beyond the actual pain. It is also done to avoid developing unsteadiness in the face for fear of the bit; for horses rotate and turn more naturally with whips than with bits.

Second, once they are made to run in pairs,[43] in addition to the spurs people strike them with the rod, to make them run more, increasing the fear of the blow of the rod above the striking of the spurs. But I would not greatly praise this custom, were it not so common; for it seems reasonable to me that if a ship's motion is impeded by moving on it, and it sails better if everyone stays still, so steadiness would be a great advantage for running the mount better, striking well only with the spurs. But since it is so much a custom, I believe that, to run more, striking with the rod does provide some aid, if we do not shake the body much with it.

Third, when horses show the vice of biting, pulling to the left, or being rebellious, people correct it in part with the stick, as I will explain hereafter, God willing, when speaking of the vices of mounts.[44]

Fourth, at moments of need, often owing to breaking of the bit or curb, or losing the bit, riders avoid great dangers with the stick,

---

[42] *chuparsse*: Horses will sometimes suck in their midsection to shy away from contact from the spur.

[43] run in pairs: *correr parelhas*. This refers to light equestrian games in which riders and their horses demonstrated their skill by running in matched pairs, possibly also throwing canes and other light projectiles. The sport was known in Spain as *correr parejas*, a phrase that still survives with figurative meaning in modern Spanish. See Andrade, *Luz*, pp. 418–25; Bañuelos y de la Cerda, *Libro de la gineta*, p. 58.

[44] This corresponds to Section 14 in Duarte's plan for this part of the book; it was never written, though this passage suggests that he was still hoping to do so as late as the final year of his life.

applying it in the face and making the horse turn to a wall or such a spot where it is held forcibly in place; and if they cannot find one, they go uphill, so that it becomes tired with the pain of the spurs; or they use it to turn aside from dangerous places. Considering these benefits that one receives at such times, it is a good custom when riding to bear a stick or rod in the hand, so that you can take advantage of it when needed.

And so I briefly make an end of this sixth part, on striking with the spurs, stick, or rod.

Here ends Section 6, and begins Section 7: Some instruction about the dangers and accidents that can happen when we are riding, and how we can protect ourselves from them, with God's grace

In this seventh part, on how riders often fall owing to the dangers and hazards that can happen from lack of awareness and good knowledge of riding, I mean to write these precepts that seem good to me, so you can be guarded against them in most instances.

You should know first of all that no human precaution is of any use at all, if it is not helped by the special grace of our Lord God. For it is written, "Neither he who plants nor he who waters, but the Lord God gives all good outcomes."[45] Therefore I neither believe nor want others to suppose that I would presume that my precepts are enough to guard securely against every harm and hazard. But as the saying goes, if you observe reason and measure in all your actions, seldom or never will you have cause to blame bad luck; so it seems good to me to offer these precepts so that everyone can help himself with them.

In this and all other things we see by ordinance of our Lord that those who know how to keep themselves from dangers appropriately suffer less harm. Therefore I believe that for this purpose it will be beneficial to know my recommendations concerning matters that I have experienced in this science and established through reason once I decided to write about it.

---

[45] I Corinthians 3:7.

You should know that there are five general ways in which we fail through ignorance of how to protect ourselves from hazards:

> First, knowing poorly how to hold ourselves on the mount, so that we are endangered by falling from it.
> Second, not being mindful or remembering to securely adjust all the gear, both of the horse and ourselves.
> Third, the mount's lameness, pain, weakness, exhaustion, bad habits or bad handling.
> Fourth, not knowing how to guard ourselves from dangers before they befall us.
> Fifth, not knowing how to remedy some situations when we find ourselves in their initial stages, from which those who are knowledgeable do save themselves with good mindfulness, by grace of the Lord.

By explaining all of this, I think that I will give good recommendations for some people; and for those who know much, I will recall to mind things they have already practiced.

As to the first, to know how we should guard against falling from the mount, return to the first part of this book where I offer many precepts on how to ride strongly; there you will find what seems to me most profitable for holding yourself strongly on the mount.

As to the second, pertaining to adjusting ourselves and the mount, in the aforementioned part I have also written about this; but recognizing that some of those things could be of great benefit in this context, I will write about them more clearly again here, which are these:

You should take heed with the bit that the leathers of the headstall and reins are good and strong, and also the fittings and rivets, in such a way that you cannot be put at risk by its failing. They should not be placed high or low, and the curb should be properly positioned, for lack of which many horses lose their bit, and their riders are put in great dangers.

The saddle should be of a good fashion, according to what you have to do in it; for sometimes riders are put at risk because it is poorly made in the arçons, or tight in the seat.

The girths should be properly checked, strong, and well adjusted.

The stirrups should not be so tight that your feet cannot come out of them, nor so broad that they slip through them or it makes you ride weakly. They should not be unreasonably long, owing to many dangers that arise from this, as experience well teaches, even though many people bear them this way for the sake of fancy and not good custom.

The spurs should be of moderate length, ensuring that they do not catch on the latigo or saddle-cover owing to their excessive length or size of the wheels.

You should not be encumbered by your garments in time of need, for some people are put at risk by them.

By these precepts I have written, everyone can advise himself in similar things pertaining to himself and his mount.

As to the third part, regarding how we should attend to lameness, pain, weakness, tiredness, bad manner or vices of the mount, one could offer various general precepts on this subject; but lords and others who can, should avoid riding such mounts, and those who do not have other horses, should run and walk them with great care according as they sense their shortcomings, being mindful of where they are going and what they may or must do on such mounts, paying attention to the hand, reins and spurs. To explain this, I will offer these examples, from which one can extrapolate other precepts.

If your mount is lame in the chest, forelegs, or forefeet, or bears down on the bit from tiredness, or strikes its sinews with its shoes, or drags its forefeet, you should be especially careful on the lower slopes of mountains, or hard or rocky ground, even if it is muddy.

If the horse bears down forward, going low in the forefeet and forelegs through deficiency or bad habit, or has trouble getting through scrub that is thick or encumbered with mud, water, or brush, you should be very cautious.

If the horse is deficient in the hindlegs, of weak loins, tries to dislodge the saddle,[46] has weak lungs, is weak or tired, or its girths slip when climbing, you should take care, for its weakness can greatly impede or hamper the rider.

If the horse drags its hindlegs, is frisky, skittish and excessively eager, you should take special care on steep paths, narrow roads, and tight passages.

---

[46] *a ssella filhem*: Meaning uncertain.

If the horse carelessly crosses its forelegs, runs foolishly, or is very lame, you should be wary of it in all kinds of places, for they are all dangerous.

You should be careful of the vices of mounts in every place and time (as I will explain hereafter, God willing, when the time comes)[47] especially in those instances that entail the greatest potential danger or disgrace.

You should be very careful on mules in mud, or rough or deep water.

You should be careful with jealous mounts, for they never lack a target and opportunity to show their vices.

If the horse does not see well, or is poorly bitted, or very lively, you should be more cautious in places thick with trees, watercourses, furrows, pits, stony hillocks, and in thunderstorms, for in such situations one cannot easily turn aside from such dangers.

If the horse runs the scrubland jumping on its forelegs with its weight forward, or puts its weight on the bit, or is weak in the forelegs, you should be especially careful of places with rabbit-warrens and very wet moors.

Deo gracias[48]

---

[47] This corresponds to Section 14 in Duarte's plan for this part of the book. See above, p. 150 fn. 44.

[48] "Thanks be to God." This is an addition by the scribe upon completing his work in copying the text.

Bibliography

Manuscripts

Paris, Bibliothèque Nationale MS portuguais 5

Editions and Translations of Duarte's Works

Duarte I, King of Portugal, *Livro da ensinança de bem cavalgar toda sela que fez El-Rey Dom Eduarte de Portugal e do Algarve e Senhor de Ceuta*, ed. Joseph M. Piel (Lisbon: Livraria Bertrand, 1944).
———, *Livro da ensinança de bem cavalgar toda sela que fez El-Rey Dom Eduarte de Portugal e do Algarve e Senhor de Ceuta*, ed. Joseph M. Piel. 2nd ed. (Lisbon: Imprensa Nacional-Casa da Moeda, 1986).
———, *The Art of Riding on Every Saddle*, transl. António Franco Preto and Luís Preto (Lexington KY: n.p., 2011).
———, *Leal Conselheiro e Livro da Ensinança de Bem Cavalgar Toda Sela*, ed. F. Costa Marques. Colecção Literária "Atlántida" (Coimbra: Atlántida, 1965).
———, *Leal conselheiro, o qual fez Dom Eduarte, Rey de Portugal e do Algarve e Senhor de Cepta*, ed. Joseph Piel (Lisbon: Livraria Bertrand, 1942).
———, *Leal conselheiro*, ed. Maria Helena Lopes de Castro and Afonso Botelho (Lisbon: Imprensa Nacional-Casa da Moeda, 1998).
———, *Livro dos Conselhos de el-Rei D. Duarte (Livro da Cartuxa)*, ed. A. H. de Oliveira Marques, João José Alves Dias, Teresa F. Rodrigues (Lisbon: Editorial Estampa, 1982).
———, *Leal Conselheiro e Livro da Ensinança de Bem Cavalgar Toda Sela*, ed. Francisco António de Campos, baron de Vila Nova de Fozcoa (Lisbon: Typografia Rollandiana, 1843).
———, *Leal Conselheiro o qual fez Dom Duarte pela graça de Deos Rei de Portugal e do Algarve e Senhor de Ceuta, a requirimento da muito excellente Rainha Dona Leonor sua mulher, seguido do livro da Ensinança de bem cavalgar toda sella, que fez o mesmo Rei, o qual começou em sendo Infante*, ed. José Ignacio Roquete (Paris: J. P. Aillaud, 1842 [1843]).

———, "Livro da Ensinança de Bem Cavalgar Toda Sela," in *Obras dos Príncipes de Avis*, ed. M. Lopes de Almeida (Porto: Lello & Irmão, 1981), 443–523.

Other Printed Works

Aguilar, Pedro de, *Tractado de la cavalleria de la gineta* (Seville: Hernando Diaz, 1572).
Albuquerque, Martim de, and Eduardo Borges Nunes, eds, *Ordenações del-Rei Dom Duarte* (Lisbon: Fundação Calouste Gulbenkian, 1988).
Alcocer, Franzisco de, *Tratado del juego... en el qual se trata copiosamente quando los jugadores pecan y son obligados a restituir... y las apuestas, suertes, torneos, iustas, juegos de cana, toros, y truhanes* (Salamanca: Andrea de Portonariis, 1559).
Allmand, Christopher, *The "De re militari" of Vegetius. The reception, transmission and legacy of a Roman text in the Middle Ages* (Cambridge: Cambridge University Press, 2011).
Almeida, Fortunato de, *História de Portugal*, 6 vols (Coimbra: Imprensa da Universidade, 1922–9).
Almeida, M. Lopes de, *Obras dos príncipes de Avis* (Porto: Lelho e Irmão, 1981).
al-Sarraf, Shihab, "Close Combat Weapons in the Early Abbasid Period: Maces, Axes, and Swords", in *Companion to Medieval Arms and Armor*, ed. David C. Nicolle (Woodbridge, Suffolk: The Boydell Press, 2002), 149–78.
Andrade, Antonia Galvam de, *Arte de cavallaria de gineta; bom primor de ferrar; e alveitaria, dividida em tres tratados, que contem varios discursos e experiencias desta Arte* (Lisbon: Joam da Costa, 1678).
Andrade, Manoel Carlos de, *Luz da liberal e nobre arte da cavallaria* (Lisbon: Regia Officina Typographica, 1790).
Anglo, Sydney, "How to Win at Tournaments: The Technique of Chivalric Combat", *Antiquaries Journal* 68.2 (1988), 248–64.
———, "Jousting – the earliest treatises", *Livrustkammaren. Journal of the Royal Armoury* (1991–92), 3–23.
———, "How to Kill a Man at Your Ease: Fencing Books and the Duelling Ethic", in *Chivalry in the Renaissance*, ed. Sydney Anglo (Woodbridge: Boydell and Brewer, 1990), 1–12.
———, *The Martial Arts of Renaissance Europe* (New Haven and London: Yale University Press, 2000).

———, "The man who taught Leonardo darts". *Antiquaries Journal* 69 (1989), 261–278.

Araújo, Yann Loïc Macedo de Morais, "Contributo para a história da alveitaria e dos cavalos de guerra no Portugal medieval – Contribution to the history of medieval Portuguese farriery (*alveitaria*)", *Revista Portuguesa de Ciências Veterinárias* 99 (2004), 19–25.

Aristotle, *The Nicomachean Ethics*, transl. Martin Ostwald (Indianapolis: Bobbs-Merrill, 1962).

Aristotle [Pseudo], *Segredo dos segredos: Tradução portuguesa, segundo um manuscrito inédito do século xv* (Lisbon: Faculdade de Letras da Universidade de Lisboa, 1960).

Asín, Jaime Oliver, "Origen Arabe de 'Rebato, Arrobda' y sus Homónimos. Contribución al Estudio de la Historia Medieval de la Táctica Militar y de su Lexico Peninsular", *Boletín de la Real Academia Española* 15 (1928), 347–95, 496–542.

Avila, Juan Arias de, *Discurso para estar a la gineta, con gracia y hermosura* (Madrid: n.p., 1590).

Ayton, Andrew, *Knights and Warhorses: Military Service and the English Aristocracy under Edward III* (Woodbridge, Suff.: Boydell Press, 1994).

Azevedo, Antonio de Sena Faria de Vasconcelos, *Contribuição para o estudo da psicología de El-Rei D. Duarte* (Lisbon: n.p., 1937).

Bachrach, Bernard S., "*Caballus* and *Caballarius* in Medieval Warfare", in *The Study of Chivalry: Resources and Approaches*, ed. Howell Chickering and Thomas H. Seiler (Kalamazoo, Mich.: Medieval Institute Publications, 1988), 173–211.

Bañuelos y de la Cerda, Luis de, *Libro de la Jineta* (Madrid: Society of Spanish Book Lovers. 1877 [1605]).

Barber, Richard, and Juliet Barker, *Tournaments. Jousts, Chivalry and Pageants in the Middle Ages* (New York: Weidenfeld & Nicolson, 1989).

Barclay, Harold R., *The Role of the Horse in Man's Culture* (London and New York: J. A. Allen, 1980).

Bascetta, Carlo, *Sport e Giuochi. Trattati e Scritti dal 15. al 18. Secolo* (Milan: Edizioni il Polifilo, 1978).

Beatie, Russel H., *Saddles* (Norman OK: University of Oklahoma Press 1981).

Bell, Aubrey F. G., *Portuguese Literature* (Oxford: Clarendon Press, 1922).

Bennett, Deb, *Conquerors: The Roots of New World Horsemanship* (Solvang CA: Amigo Publications, 1998).

Bertrandon de la Broquière, *Le Voyage d'Outremer*, ed. C. Schefer (Paris: Ernest Leroux, 1892).

Bibliothèque Nationale, Département des Manuscrits, *Catalogue des Manuscrits Espagnols et des Manuscrits Portugais*, ed. M. Alfred Morel-Fatio (Paris: Imprimerie Nationale, 1892).

Blundeville, Thomas, *A newe booke containing the arte of ryding, and breakinge greate horses*. (London: W. Seres, 1561[?]).

Blundeville, Thomas, *The fower chiefyst offices belonging to horsemanshippe* (London: W. Seres, 1580).

Boeheim, Wendelin, *Handbuch der Waffenkunde* (Graz: Akademische Druck- und Verlagsanstalt, 1966).

Botelho, Afonso, "Andar dereito. Considerações sobre a 'Cavalaria' segundo D. Duarte", *Revista Portuguesa de Filosofia* 7:3 (1951), 253–74.

Botelho, Afonso, *Dom Duarte*. Pensamento Português 4 (Lisbon and São Paulo: Verbo, 1991).

Bourdon, Léon, "Question de priorité autour de la découverte du manuscript du 'Leal conselheiro'", *Arcquivos do Centro Cultural Português* 14 (1979), 3–26.

Brito, Bernardo de, *Elógios Historicos dos Senhores Reis de Portugal* (Lisbon: Typografia Rollandiana, 1786).

Bueil, Jean de, *Le Jouvencel*, ed. C. Favre and L. Lecestre (Paris: Librarie Renouard, 1887–89).

Cartagena, Alonso de, *Libros de Tulio: De senetute; De los ofiçios*, ed. María Morrás (Alcalá de Henares: Universidad de Alcalá de Henares, 1996).

———, *Memorial de virtudes*, ed. Mar Campos Souto (Burgos: Instituto Municipal de Cultura, Ayuntamiento de Burgos, 2004).

Cassian, Saint John (Johannes Cassianus), *The Conferences*, transl. Boniface Ramsey (New York: Paulist Press, 1997).

Cassian, Saint John (Johannes Cassianus), *Collationes*, in *Johannes Cassiani Opera Omnia*, ed. J.-P. Migne. *Patrologia Latina* 49 (Paris: Garnier Frères, 1874), 1.477–1328.

Castiglione, Baldesar, *The Book of the Courtier*, ed. Daniel Javitch (New York and London: Norton, 2002).

———, *Il Cortegiano* (Venice: Bernardo Basa, 1584).

Castro, Maria Lopes de, "Leal Conselheiro: Itinerário do Manuscrito", *Penelope* 16 (1996), 109–24.

Cavalheiro, António Rodrigues, "D. Duarte e a versatilidade historiográfica", *Ocidente* 37.136 (1949), 92–95.

Cavendish, William, Duke of Newcastle, *A new method, and extraordinary invention, to dress horses, and work them according to nature* (London: T. Milbourn, 1667).

Ceballos-Escalera y Gila, Alfonso, *La orden y divisa de la Banda Real de Castilla* (Madrid: Prensa y Ediciones Iberoamericanas, 1993).

Cepeda, Isabel Vilares, *Bibliografia da Prosa Medieval em Língua Portuguesa* (Lisbon: Ministério da Cultura, Instituto da Biblioteca Nacional e do Livro, 1995).

Cespedes y Velasco, Francisco de, *Tratado de la Gineta* (Lisbon: Luys Estupiñan, 1609).

Chacón, Hernán, *Tractado de la cavallería de la gineta*, ed. Noel Fallows (Exeter: University of Exeter Press, 1999).

Chénière, Ernest, "Étude des mors aux XVIe et XVIIe siècles dans les traités de Pavari, Fiaschi, La Broue et La Noue", in *Les arts de l'équitation dans l'Europe de la Renaissance. VIe colloque de l'Ecole nationale d'équitation au château d'Oiron (4 et 5 octobre 2002)*, ed. Patrice Franchet d'Espèrey, Monique Chatenet, and Ernest Chenière (Arles: Actes Sud, 2009), 79–92.

Chevenix-Trench, Charles, *A History of Horsemanship* (Garden City NY: Doubleday and Co, 1970).

Cicero, Marcus Tullius, *Livro dos ofícios*, transl. Pedro, Infante of Portugal; ed. Joseph Maria Piel (Coimbra: Universidade, 1948).

Clark, John, ed., *The Medieval Horse and its Equipment, c. 1150 – c. 1450*. Medieval Finds from Excavations in London 5 (Woodbridge, Suffolk: Boydell Press, 2004).

Clephan, Robert Coltman, *The Tournament: Its Periods and Phases* (London: Methuen, 1919).

Cram, David, Jeffrey L. Forgeng, and Dorothy Johnston, *Francis Willughby's Book of Games: A Seventeenth-Century Treatise on Sports, Games, and Pastimes* (Aldershot and Burlington VT: Ashgate, 2003).

Cruso, John, *Military Instructions for Cavalry* (Cambridge: by the printers of the University, 1632).

Cummins, J. G., *The Hound and the Hawk: The Art of Medieval Hunting* (New York, St. Martin's Press, 1988).

Cuneo, Pia F., "Das Reiten als Kriegstechnink, als Sport und als Kunst: die Körpertechnik des Reitens und gesellschaftliche Identität im frühneuzeitlichen Deutschland", in *Bewegtes Leben. Körpertechniken in der Frühen Neuzeit*, ed. Rebekka von Mallinckrodt (Wolfenbüttel: Herzog August Bibliothek Wolfenbüttel, 2008), 167–87.

Cuneo, Pia F., "Just a Bit of Control: The Historical Significance of Sixteenth – and Seventeenth-Century German Bit-Books", in *The Culture of the Horse: Status, Discipline and Identity in the Early Modern World*, ed. Karen Raber and Treva J. Tucker. Early Modern Cultural Studies (New York: Palgrave Macmillan, 2005), 141–73.

dall'Agocchie, Giovanni, *Dell'arte di scrimia Libri tre* (Venice: Giulio Tamborino, 1572).

Davenport, Millia, *The Book of Costume* (New York: Crown Publishers, 1948).

Davis, R. H. C., *The Medieval Warhorse. Origin, Development and Redevelopment* (London: Thames and Hudson, 1989).

Deblaise, Philippe, "Itinéraire du livre dans l'Europe de la Renaissance", in *Les arts de l'équitation dans l'Europe de la Renaissance. VIe colloque de l'Ecole nationale d'équitation au château d'Oiron (4 et 5 octobre 2002)*, ed. Patrice Franchet d'Espèrey, Monique Chatenet, and Ernest Chenière (Arles: Actes Sud, 2009), 253–65.

Deblaise, Philippe, *De Rusius à La Broue: Itinéraire du Livre Équestre dans l'Europe de la Renaissance* (n.p.: Philippica, 2002).

Delcampe [Escuyer de la grande Escurie du Roy], *L'art de monter à cheval. Qui monstre la belle & facile methode de se rendre bon homme de cheval* (Paris: Jacques le Gras, 1658).

Demmin, Auguste, *An Illustrated History of Arms and Armour from the Earliest Period to the Present Time* (London and New York: Bell & Sons, 1894).

Demmin, Auguste, *Die Kriegswaffen in ihren geschichtlichen Entwickelungen von den ältesten Zeiten bis auf die Gegenwart: eine Encyklopädie der Waffenkunde* (Leipzig: P. Friesehahn, 1893).

Descoins, Eduard, *Arab Equitation: Its Principles Its Practice*, transl. James E. Luck (Philadelphia: Xlibris Corp. 2007).

Dias, Maria Isabel Rosa, *A Arte de ser Bom Cavaleiro*. Letras 10 (Lisbon: Editorial Estampa, 1997).

Dillon, Viscount, "On a MS Collection of Ordinances of Chivalry of the Fifteenth Century," *Archaeologia* 57 (1900), 29–70.

Dinis, António Joaquim, ed., *Monumenta Henricina*, 15 vols (Coimbra: Commissão Executiva das Comemorações do Quinto Centenário da Morte do Infante D. Henrique, 1960–74).

Dionísio, João, "A recepção de D. Duarte no séc. XX", in *Sobre o Tempo: Secção Portuguesa da AHLM, Actas do III Colóquio*, ed. Paulo Meneses (Ponta Delgada: Universidade dos Açores, 2001), 361–75.

Dionísio, João, "Do *Memoriale Virtutum*, de Alfonso de Cartagena, ao *Leal Conselheiro*, de D. Duarte", *Caligrama* 9 (2004), 261–80.

Drugmand, Pierre, "L'éperonnerie", in *Les arts de l'équitation dans l'Europe de la Renaissance. VIe colloque de l'Ecole nationale d'équitation au château d'Oiron (4 et 5 octobre 2002)*, ed. Patrice Franchet d'Espèrey, Monique Chatenet, and Ernest Chenière (Arles: Actes Sud, 2009), 68–78.

Duarte, Luis Miguel, *D. Duarte, requiem por um rei triste* (Lisbon: Circulo de Leitores, 2005).

Fallows, Noel, "Alfonso de Cartagena", in *Dictionary of Literary Bibliography, vol. 286: Castilian Writers, 1400–1500*, ed. Frank A. Domínguez and George D. Greenia (Detroit: Gale, 2004), 3–14.

Fallows, Noel, *Jousting in Medieval and Renaissance Iberia* (Woodbridge: Boydell and Brewer, 2010).

Fallows, Noel, *Un texto inédito sobre la caballería del Renacimiento español: "Doctrina del arte de la cauallería," de Juan Quijada de Reayo* (Liverpool: Liverpool University Press, 1996).

Fallows, Noel, *The Chivalric Vision of Alfonso de Cartagena: Study and Edition of the* Doctrinal de los caualleros (Newark DE: Juan de la Cuesta, 1995).

Felton, Sidney, *Masters of Equitation* (London: J. A. Allen, 1962).

Fernandes, Rogério, "D. Duarte e a educação senhorial", *Vértice* 396–7 (1977), 347–88.

Fernandez de Andrada, Pedro, *De la naturaleza del cavallo* (Seville: Fernando Dias, 1580).

Folger Shakespeare Library, *The Reign of the Horse: The Horse in Print, 1500–1715. An Exhibition Prepared by Elizabeth Niemyer* (Washington DC: Folger Shakespeare Library, 1991).

Fontaine, Marie-Madeleine, *Le condottiere Pietro del Monte, philosophe et écrivain de la Renaissance, 1457–1509* (Geneva and Paris: Slatkine, 1991).

Fontaine, Marie Madeleine, "La voltige à cheval chez Pietro Del Monte (1492 et 1509), Rabelais (1535) et Montaigne (1580–1592)", in *Les arts de l'équitation dans l'Europe de la Renaissance. VIe colloque de l'Ecole nationale d'équitation au château d'Oiron (4 et 5 octobre 2002)*, ed. Patrice Franchet d'Espèrey, Monique Chatenet, and Ernest Chenière (Arles: Actes Sud, 2009), 197–252.

Forgeng, J. L. and Alexander Kiermayer, "'The Chivalric Art': German Martial Arts Treatises of the Middle Ages and Renaissance", in *The Cutting Edge: Studies in Ancient and Medieval Combat*, ed. E. B. Molloy (Stroud, Gloucs.: Tempus, 2007), 153–67.

Forgeng, Jeffrey L. and Will McLean, *Daily Life in Chaucer's England*. 2nd ed. (Westport CT and London: Greenwood Press, 2009).

Forgeng, Jeffrey L. "'Owning the Art': The German Fechtbuch Tradition", in *The Noble Art of the Sword: Fashion and Fencing in Renaissance Europ. 1520–1630*, ed. Tobias Capwell (London: Paul Holberton/The Wallace Collection, 2012), 164–75.

Forgeng, Jeffrey L. "Pietro Monte's *Exercises* and the Medieval Science of Arms", in *The Armorer's Art: Essays in Honor of Stuart Pyhrr*, ed. Donald J. La Rocca (Woonsocket, RI: Mowbray Publishing, 2014), 107–14.

Forgeng, Jeffrey L. *The Art of Swordsmanship by Hans Lecküchner* (Woodbridge, Suffolk: Boydell and Brewer, 2015).

Fouquet, Samuel, sieur de Beaurepaire, *Traitté des embouchures... L'art de monter à cheval et de dresser les chevaux* (Paris: Jacques de Gras, 1663).

Fuchs, Barbara, *Exotic Nation: Maurophilia and the Construction of Early Modern Spain* (Philadelphia: University of Pennsylvania Press, 2009).

Gaier, Claude, "Technique des combats singuliers d'après les auteurs 'bourguignons' du XVe siècle", *Le Moyen Age* 92 (1986), 5–40.

Gallardo, Luis Fernández, *Alonso de Cartagena. Una biografía política en la Castilla del siglo XV* (Valladolid: Junta de Castilla y León, 2002).

Gallego, Fr. Pedro, *Tratado da cavallaria de gineta ordenado de vinte e quarto preguntas que um curioso lhe mandou preguntar* (Lisbon: Pedro Crasbeck, 1629).

Gama, José, *A filosofia da cultura portuguesa no "Leal conselheiro" de D. Duarte* (Lisbon: Fundação Calouste Gulbenkian, 1995).

Gama, José, "A geração de Avis. I: D. Duarte", in *História do Pensamento Filosófico Português*, ed. Pedro Calafate (Lisbon: Caminho, 1999), 379–411.

Gavilanes Laso, José Luis, "Los libros de montería medievales hispanoportugueses", in *Actas de Congreso Internacional de Historia y Cultura en la Frontera –1er Encuentro de Lusitanistas Españoles (1999)* (Cáceres: Universidad de Extremadura, 2000), 89–115.

Gavilanes Laso, José Luis, "La prosa profana, didáctica y doctrinal del siglo XV", in *Historia de la literatura portuguesa*, ed. José Luis Gavilanes Laso and António Apolinário (Madrid: Cátedra, 2000), 137–38.

Gelbhaar, Axel, *Mittelalterliches und frühneuzeitliches Reit- und Fahrzubehör aus dem Besitz der Kunstsammlungen der Veste Coburg. Documenta Hippologica* (Hildesheim, Zürich, New York: Olms Presse, 1997).

Giese, Wilhelm, "Portugiesisches Reitzeug am Anfange des XV. Jahrhunderts, nach D. Duartes 'Livro da Ensinança de bem cavalgar toda sella'", in *Miscélanea científica e literária dedicada ao dr. Leite de Vasconcelos* (Coimbra: Universidade, 1934), 67–84.

Giles of Rome (Aegidius Romanus), *De Regimine Principum Libri III* (Frankfurt: Minerva GMBH, 1968).

Gillmeister, Heiner, *Tennis: A Cultural History* (New York: New York University Press, 1998).

Gillmor, Carroll, "Practical Chivalry: The Training of Horses for Tournaments and Warfare", *Studies in Medieval and Renaissance History* 13 (1992), 7–29.

Gilmour, Lauren Adams, ed., *In the Saddle: An Exploration of the Saddle through History. A meeting of the Archaeological Leather Group at Saddlers' Hall, London, 23 October 2002* (London: Archetype Publications, 2004).

Gladitz, Charles, *Horse Breeding in the Medieval World* (Dublin: Four Courts Press, 1997).
Glorious Horsemen: Equestrian Art in Europe, 1500–1800 (Springfield, Mass: Museum of Fine Arts, 1981).
Gomes, Rita Costa, *The Making of a Court Society: Kings and Nobles in Late Medieval Portugal* (Cambridge: Cambridge University Press, 2003).
Greenfield, Sidney M., "The Patrimonial State and Patron-Client Relations in Iberia and Latin America: Sources of 'The System' in the Fifteenth-Century Writings of the Infante D. Pedro of Portugal", *Ethnohistory* 24:2 (Spring 1977), 163–78.
Grisone, Federico, *The Rules of Riding*, ed. and transl. Elizabeth MacKenzie Tobey and Federica Brunori Deigan (Tempe AZ: Arizona Center for Medieval and Renaissance Studies, 2012).
Grancsay, Stephen V., *Equestrian Equipment, Mainly Medieval and Renaissance: A Loan Exhibition of Equestrian Equipment from the Metropolitan Museum of Art* (Louisville, KY: J. B. Speed Art Museum, 1955).
Harris, Max, *Aztecs, Moors, and Christians: Festivals of Reconquest in Mexico and Spain* (Austin: University of Texas Press, 2000).
Hewitt, Herbert James, *The Horse in Medieval England* (London: J.A. Allen, 1983).
Hick, Steve, "Dom Duarte and his Advice on Swordsmanship", in *Spada: An Anthology of Swordsmanship in Memory of Ewart Oakeshott* (Union City, CA: Chivalry Bookshelf, 2002), 65–69.
Hickling, Lynda, "The Saddle of Henry V at Westminster Abbey Library", in *In the Saddle: An Exploration of the Saddle through History. A meeting of the Archaeological Leather Group at Saddlers' Hall, London, 23 October 2002*, ed. Lauren Adams Gilmour (London: Archetype Publications, 2004), 39–41.
Horst, Koert van der. *Great Books on Horsemanship: Bibliotheca Hippologica Johan Dejager* (Leiden: Brill, 2014).
Holme, Randle, *An Academie of Armory, Or, a Storehouse of Armory and Blazon* (Chester: for the author, 1688).
Hobusch, Erich, *Fair Game: A History of Hunting, Shooting, and Animal Conservation* (New York: Arco, 1980).
Huber, Michaël, "L'art du combat à cheval aux XIVe et XVe siècles dans le Saint Empire Romain Germanique, d'après les traités d'escrime", in *Maîtres et techniques de combat à la fin du Moyen Âge et au début de la Renaissance*, ed. Fabrice Cognot (Paris: Association pour l'Edition et la Diffusion des Etudes Historiques, 2006), 9–64.
Huth, Frederick Henry, *Works on Horses and Equitation. A Bibliographical Record of Hippology* (London: Bernard Quaritch, 1887).

Hyland, Ann, *The Medieval Warhorse from Byzantium to the Crusades* (London: Grange Books, 1994).
Hyland, Ann, *The Warhorse 1250–1600* (Stroud, Gloucs.: Sutton, 1998).
Hyland, Ann, "The Medieval War Saddle and its Accessories", in *In the Saddle: An Exploration of the Saddle through History. A meeting of the Archaeological Leather Group at Saddlers' Hall, London, 23 October 2002*, ed. Lauren Adams Gilmour (London: Archetype Publications, 2004), 31–38.
Ibn Hudhayl [Aly ben Abderrahman ben Hodeil el Andalusy], *La parure des cavaliers et l'insigne des preux*, transl. Louis Mercer (Paris: Librarie Orientaliste Paul Gauthier, 1924).
Imbotti de Beaumont, Louis, *L'escuier françois, qui enseigne à monter à cheval et à voltiger* (Paris: Veuve Beaumont, 1679).
João I, King of Portugal, *Livro da montaria feito por D. João I de Portugal*, ed. Francisco M. Esteves Pereira (Coimbra: Universidade, 1918).
Jordani Ruffi Calabriensis Hippiatria, ed. Girolamo Molin (Padua: Typis Seminarii, 1818).
Khorasani, Manouchehr Moshtagh, *Persian Archery and Swordsmanship: Historical Martial Arts of Iran* (Frankfurt: Niloufar Books, 2013).
Kreutzberger, Hans, *Warhaftige und Eygentliche Contrafactur und Formen der Zeumen und gebis zu allerley mängeln unnd unterrichtung der Pferdt* (Augsburg: n.p., 1562).
Lacy, Charles de Lacy, *The History of the Spur* (London: The Connoisseur/ Otto Limited, 1911).
Laking, Guy Francis, Sir, *A Record of European Armour and Arms through Seven Centuries... with an introduction by the Baron de Cosson* (London: G. Bell and Sons, 1920–22).
Lalande, D., ed., *Le Livre des fais du bon messire Jehan le Maingre, dit Bouciquaut, mareschal de France et gouverneur de Jennes* (Geneva: Droz, 1985).
Lapa, Manuel Rodrigues, "D. Duarte e a Prosa Didactica", in *Lições de Literatura Portuguesa (Época Medieval)* (Lisbon: Centro de Estudos Filológicos, 1934), 247–71.
Lapa, Manuel Rodrigues, *Dom Duarte e os Prosadores da Casa de Avis* (Lisbon: Textos Literários, 1957).
Leão, Duarte Nunez do, *Crónicas dos reis de Portugal*, ed. Manuel Lopes de Almeida (Porto: Lello e Irmão, 1975).
Leguina y Vidal, Enrique de, *Libros de Esgrima, Españoles y Portugueses* (Madrid: Los Huerfanon, 1891).
Leguina y Vidal, Enrique de, *Bibliographia e Historia de la Esgrima Española* (Madrid: Fortanent, 1904).

Liedtke, Walter A., *Royal Horse and Rider: Painting, Sculpture, and Horsemanship 1500–1800* (New York: Abaris Books in association with the Metropolitan Museum of Art, 1990).
Lopes, Fernão, *Chronica de El-Rei D. João I*. Bibliotheca de clássicos portugueses. 7 vols. (Lisboa: Escriptorio, 1897–1898).
Lorenzo, Ramón, "Livro da Ensinança de Bem Cavalgar Toda Sela", in *Dicionário da Literatura Medieval Galega e Portuguesa*, ed. Giulia Lanciani and Giuseppe Tavani (Lisbon: Caminho, 1993), 400–2.
Lorenzo, Ramón, "*Livro de Alveitaria* de Mestre Giraldo", in *Dicionário da Literatura Medieval Galega e Portuguesa*, ed. G. Lanciani and G. Tavani (Lisbon: Caminho, 1993), 405–6.
Lorenzo, Ramón, "*Tratado de Alveitaria*", in *Dicionário da Literatura Medieval Galega e Portuguesa*, ed. Giulia Lanciani and Giuseppe Tavani (Lisbon: Caminho, 1993), 635.
Lourie, Elena, "A Society Organized for War: Medieval Spain", *Past and Present* 35 (1966), 54–76 .
Machuca, Don Bernardo de Vargas, *Teorica y exercicios de la Gineta* (Madrid: Diego Flamenco, 1619). Ed. in Sanz Egaña, *Tres Libros de Jineta*, pp. 113–270.
Madden, D. H., *A Chapter of Mediaeval History: The Fathers of the Literature of Field Sport and Horses* (London: John Murray, 1924).
Malipiero, Massimo, ed., *Il Fior di battaglia di Fiore dei Liberi da Cividale* (Ribis: Campofòrmido, 2006).
Manzanas, Eugenio, *Libro de enfrenamientos de la gineta* (Toledo: F. de Guzmán, 1570).
Markham, Gervase, *Cavelarice, or the English horseman* (London: Edward White, 1607).
Marques, A. H. de Oliveira, *Portugal na Crise dos Séculos XIV e XV* (Lisbon: Presença, 1987).
Marques, A. H. de Oliveira, *A Sociedade Medieval Portuguesa: Aspectos de Vida Quotidiana* (5th edn, Lisbon: Sá da Costa, 1987).
Marques, A. H. de Oliveira, *Guia do estudante de história medieval portuguesa* (3rd edn, Lisbon: Editorial Estampa, 1988).
Marques, F. Costa, *Leal Conselheiro e Livro da Ensinança de Bem Cavalgar. Notícia histórica e literária, selecção e anotações* (Lisbon: Livraria Clássica Editora, 1942).
Martins, Mário, *A Bíblia na Literatura Medieval Portuguesa*. Biblioteca Breve, Série literatura 35 (Lisbon: Instituto de Cultura, 1979).
Martins, Oliveira, *Os filhos de D. João I* (Lisbon: Guimarães & Cia., 1983).
McClelland, John, "Ball games, from the Roman Gentleman to the Renaissance Warrior", in *Militarism, Sport, Europe. War Without Weapons. The*

European Sports History Review 5, ed. J. A. Mangan (London: Frank Cass, 2003), 46–64.

McClelland, John, *Body and Mind: Sport in Europe from the Roman Empire to the Renaissance* (London and New York: Routledge, 2007).

Melzo, Francesco Ludovico, *Las Reglas militares sobre el govierno y servicio particular de la cavellaria*, transl. Galdericus Gali (Milan: I.B. Bidelo, 1619).

Mercier, Louis, "Les écoles espagnoles dites de la Brida et de la Gineta", *Revue de Cavalerie* 7 (1927), 301–15.

Mondschein, Ken, *The Knightly Art of Battle* (Los Angeles: The J. Paul Getty Museum, 2011).

Monte, Pietro, *De Dignoscendis Hominibus* (Milan: A. Zarotus, 1492).

Monte, Pietro, *Exercitiorum atque Artis Militaris Collectanea in Tres Libros Distincta* (Milan: Giovan'Angelo Scinzenzeler, 1509).

Monteiro, João Gouveia, *A Guerra em Portugal nos finais da idade media*. 2 vols (Lisbon: Editorial Notícias, 1998).

Moreno, H. Baquero, *Itinerários de El-Rei D. Duarte (1433–1438)* (Lisbon: Academía Portuguesa da História, 1976).

Navarrete, Francisco Perez de, *Arte de enfrenar* (Madrid: I. Gonçalez, 1626).

Nickel, Helmut, "The Tournament: An Historical Sketch", in *The Study of Chivalry: Resources and Approaches*, ed. Howell Chickering and Thomas H. Seiler (Kalamazoo, Mich., Medieval Institute Publications, 1988), 213–262.

Pacheco, Francisco Pinto, *Tratado de cavallaria da gineta, com a doctrina dos melhores authores* (Lisbon: Joam da Costa, 1670).

Palau Claveras, Agustín, *Bibliografía hispánica de veterinaria y equitación anterior a 1901* (Madrid: Imprenta Industrial, 1973).

Pedro, Infante of Portugal, and Fr. João Verba, *O Livro da Virtuosa Bemfeitoria do Infante Dom Pedro*, ed. Joaquim Costa. 3rd ed. (Porto: Empresa Industrial Gráfica do Porto, 1947).

Pedro, Infante of Portugal, and Fr. João Verba, *O Livro da Virtuosa Bemfeitoria*, in *Obras dos príncipes de Avis*, ed. M. Lopes de Almeida (Porto: Lelho e Irmão, 1981), 525–763.

Pedro, Infante of Portugal, and Fr. João Verba, *Livro da Vertuosa Benfeytoria*, ed. Adelino de Almeida Calado (Coimbra: Universidade de Coimbra, 1994).

Pedro, Infante of Portugal, *Livros dos Oficios de Marco Tullio Ciceram*, in *Obras dos príncipes de Avis*, ed. M. Lopes de Almeida (Porto: Lelho e Irmão, 1981), 765–884.

Pedro, Susana Tavares, "Apontamentos para uma descrição codicológica do códice BnF, Portugais 5", *eHumanista Journal of Iberian Studies* 22 (2012), 65–111.
Pereira Rego, António, *Instruçaõ da Cavallaria da Brida com hum copioso tratado da Alveitaria* (Coimbra: n.p., 1679, 1712).
Pereira, Carlos Henriques, "Le cheval, l'art et la littérature équestre portugaise au Moyen Âge. Présentation des œuvres équestres de Mestre Giraldo et El Rei Dom Duarte", in *L'épopée romane. Actes du XVe Congrès international Rencesvals*, ed. Gabriel Bianciotto and Claudio Galderisi. Civilisation Médiévale 13 (Poitiers: Université de Poitiers, 2002), 2.979–91.
Pereira, Carlos Henriques, *A la découverte de l'équitation portugaise* (Paris: Harmattan, 2002).
Pereira, Carlos Henriques, *Etude du premier traité d'équitation portugais: Livro da ensinança de bem cavalgar toda sela, du roi Dom Duarte* (Paris: Harmattan, 2001).
Pereira, Carlos Henriques, *Naissance et Renaissance de l'Equitation Portuguaise: Une approche historique de la Civilisation du Cheval au Portugal du XVème au XVIIIème siècle d'après l'étude des textes fondateurs de l'art equestre portuguais* (Paris: Harmattan, 2001).
Pereira, Carlos Henriques, "Le traité du roi D. Duarte: l'équitation portugaise à l'aube de la Renaissance", in *Les arts de l'équitation dans l'Europe de la Renaissance. VIe colloque de l'Ecole nationale d'équitation au château d'Oiron (4 et 5 octobre 2002)*, ed. Patrice Franchet d'Espèrey, Monique Chatenet, and Ernest Chenière (Arles: Actes Sud, 2009), 140–50.
Pereira, G., "Livro d'Alveitaria do Mestre Giraldo", *Revista Lusitana* 12:12 (1909), 1–60.
Perkins, Juliet, "Of Horses and Humours", in *A Primavera toda para ti. Homenagem a Helder Macedo. A Tribute to Helder Macedo*, ed. Teresa Cristina Cerdeira, Margarida Calafate Ribeiro, Juliet Perkins, Phillip Rothwell. Diversos 36 (Lisbon: Presença, 2004), 69–73.
Phoebus, Gaston, *The Hunting Book* (Fribourg-Geneva: Minerva, 1978–84).
Pina, Rui de, *Chronica do Senhor Rey D. Duarte*, in *Crónicas de Rui de Pina*, ed. M. Lopes de Almeida (Porto: Lello & Irmão, 1977), 487–575.
Pina, Rui de, *Crónica do Rei D. Duarte*, ed. António Borges Coelho (Lisbon: Editorial Presença, 1966).
Pluvinel, Antoine de, *The Maneige Royal* (London: J. Allen., 1989).
Puertocarrero, Juan Arias Davila, Conde de Puñorosto, *Discurso... para estar a la Gineta con gracia y hermosura* (Madrid: Pedro Madrigal, 1590). Ed. in Sanz Egaña, *Tres Libros de Jineta*, pp. 1–66.
René, duke of Anjou and king of Sicily, *Traité de la forme et devis d'un tournoi* (Paris: Verve, 1946).

Riquer, Martín de, "Las armas en el *Victorial*", in *Caballeros medievales y sus armas* (Madrid: Instituto Universitario General Gutiérrez Mellado-UNED, 1999), 163–95.

Russell, Sir Peter, *Prince Henry "the Navigator": A Life* (New Haven and London: Yale University Press, 2000).

Russell, Sir Peter, "Terá havido uma tradução medieval portuguesa do Epitome rei militaris de Vegécio?", *Euphrosyne* 29 (2001), 247–56.

Salazar, Abdón M., "El impacto humanístico de las misiones diplomáticas de Alonso de Cartagena en la Corte de Portugal entre medievo y renacimiento (1421–31)," in *Medieval Hispanic Studies Presented to Rita Hamilton*, ed. A.D. Deyermond (London: Tamesis, 1976), 215–26.

Santarém, Visconde de, "Noticia dos Manuscriptos pertencentes ao Direito Publico Externo Diplomatico de Portugal e á Historia e Litteratura do mesmo paiz que existem na Bibliotheca Real de París e outras da mesma capital, e nos archivos de França", *Annaes das Sciencias, das Artes, e das Letras* 15 pt. 2 (1821), 5–36.

Santos, Domingo Maurício Gomes, *D. Duarte e as responsabilidades de Tânger (1433–38)* (Lisbon: Editora Gráfica Portuguesa, 1960).

Sanz Egaña, C., ed., *Tres Libros de Jineta de los Siglos XVI y XVII* (Madrid: Sociedad de Bibliófilos Españoles, 1951).

Schmidt, Sandra, "Trois dialogues de l'exercise de sauter et voltiger en l'air: Strategies of Ennoblement of a Bodily Practice in the Sixteenth Century", in *Sport and Culture in Early Modern Europe; Le Sport dans la Civilisation de l'Europe Pré-Moderne*, ed. John McClelland and Brian Merilees (Toronto: Center for Reformation and Renaissance Studies, 2009), 377–89.

Serrão, Joel, ed., *Dicionário de História de Portugal*, 6 vols (Oporto: Livraria Figueirinhas, 1992).

Silva, Candido José Xavier Dias da, "Acerca do 'Leal Conselheiro' d'El-Rei D. Duarte, e do 'Livro da ensinança de bem cavalgar'", *Annaes das Sciencias, das Artes e das Letras*. 8 pt. 1, 9 pt. 1 (Apr–Jul 1820), 3–24, 92–118.

Simões, Manuel G., "Os textos didácticos da 'Geração de Avis'", in *História da Literatura Portuguesa* I, ed. Francisco Lyon de Castro (Lisbon: Publicações Alfa, 2001), 389–410.

Smith, G. Rex, *Medieval Muslim Horsemanship: A Fourteenth-Century Arabic Cavalry Manual*. British Library Booklets (London: British Library, 1979).

Sousa Viterbo, Francisco Marques de, *A Esgrima em Portugal: Subsidios para a sua Historia* (Lisbon: Manoel Gomes, 1899).

Stokes, William, *The Vaulting Master, or, The art of vaulting* (London: I. Okes, 1641).

Stradanus, Johannes (Jan van der Straet), *"Nova Reperta", New Discoveries of the Middle Ages and the Renaissance* (Norwalk, Conn.: Burndy Library, 1953).
Suarez de Peralta, Juan, *Tractado de la cavalleria de la gineta y brida* (Seville: Fernando Díaz, 1580).
Tapia y Salzedo, Gregorio de, *Exercicios de Gineta* (Madrid: Diego Diaz, 1643).
Tavard, Christian-Henry, *Sattel und Zaumzeug: Das Pferdegeschirr in Vergangenheit und Gegenwart* (Köln: Verlag M. Dumont Schauberg, 1975).
Tobler, Christian Henry, *Captain of the Guild: Master Peter Falkner's Art of Knightly Defense* (Wheaton IL: Freelance Academy Press, 2011).
Tomassini, Giovanni Battista, *The Italian Tradition of Equestrian Art: A Survey of the Treatises on Horsemanship from the Renaissance and the Centuries Following* (Franktown VA: Xenophon Press, 2014).
Torrecilla, Andrés Avelino, Marqués de la, *Índice de bibliografía hípica española y portuguesa, catalogada alfabéticamente por orden de autores y por orden títulos de las obras* (Madrid: Rivadeneyra, 1916–1921).
Unterkircher, F., *King René's Book of Love (Le Cueur d'Amours Espris)* (New York: George Braziller, 1980).
Vadi, Filippo, *[De] Arte Gladiatoria: 15th Century Swordsmanship of Master Filippo Vadi*, ed. Gregory Mele and Luca Porzio (Union City CA: Chivalry Bookshelf, 2003).
Vargas Machucha, Bernardo de, *Libro de exercicios de la gineta* (Madrid: P. Madrigal, 1600).
Vasconcelos, C. M. de, "Mestre Giraldo e os seus tratados de Alveitaria e Cetraria", *Revista Lusitana* 13 (1910), 149–73.
Vasconcelos, C. M. de, "Livro dalveitaria pera qualquer besta que quiserdes", *Revista Lusitana* 12 (1909), 110–78.
Vieyra, Anthony, *Dictionary of the Portuguese and English Languages*. 2 vols (London: J. Collingwood et al., 1827).
Villalobos y Benavides, Simón de, *Modo de pelear á la gineta* (Valladolid: Andrés de Merchan, 1606). Ed. in Sanz Egaña, *Tres Libros de Jineta*, pp. 67–112.
Walker, Elaine, "'The Author of their Skill': Human and Equine Understanding in the Duke of Newcastle's 'New Method'", in *The Horse as Cultural Icon: The Real and Symbholic Horse in the Early Modern World*, ed. Peter Edwards, Elspeth Graham and Karl A. E. Enenkel. Intersections: Interdisciplinary Studies in Early Modern Culture 18 (Leiden: Brill, 2011), 327–50.
Wallhausen, Johann Jacob, *Ritterkunst* (Graz: Akademische Druck – u. Verlagsanstalt, 1969).

Wells, E. B., *Horsemanship: A Bibliography of Printed Materials from the Sixteenth Century through 1974* (New York: Garland, 1985).
Xenophon, *The Art of Horsemanship*, transl. Morris H. Morgan (Boston: Little, Brown, and Co. 1893).
Zschille, Richard and Robert Forrer, *Die Pferdetrense in ihrer Formen-Entwicklung. Ein Versuch zur Characterisirung und Datirung der Mundstücke der Pferdezäumung unserer Kulturvölker* (Berlin: Paul Bette, 1893).
Zschille, Richard and Robert Forrer, *Der Sporn in seiner Formen-Entwicklung. Ein Versuch zur Characterisirung und Datirung der Sporen unserer Kulturvölker* (Berlin: Paul Bette, 1891).
Zschille, Richard and Robert Forrer, *Reitersporen aus Zwanzig Jahrhunderten. Eine Waffengeschichtliche Studie* (Berlin: Paul Bette, 1899).
Zschille, Richard and Robert Forrer, *Die Steigbugel in ihrer Formen-Entwicklung. Characterisirung und Datirung der Steigbügel unserer Culturvölker* (Berlin: Paul Bette, 1896).
Zurara, Gomes Eannes de, *Crónica da Tomada de Ceuta por el Rei D. João I*, ed. Francisco M. Pereira (Lisbon: Academia das Sciencias, 1915).

Index

adarga 28, 39; *see also* shield
Afonso V 7
Andrade, Manuel Carlos 9
arções 20, 28, 60, 61, 64, 69, 71–72, 76, 103, 152; *see also* saddle
Aristotle 5, 17, 98 fn. 5, 99
armor 36, 41, 51, 73, 97, 101, 103, 104, 107, 112, 127, 132, 135, 149; *see also* helm; shield; vamplate
Avis dynasty 3, 7
bear 123, 124, 126, 127, 128
Bible 47, 151
bit 13, 22–25, 27, 28, 57, 58, 70, 76 fn. 27, 94, 110, 111, 112, 152, 159
    scatch-bit 25, 111
    tari bit 25, 111
boar 123, 124, 126, 128
brida riding 1, 7, 27–28, 59; *see also* jennet riding and equipment
bridle 23, 152; *see also* bit; curb; reins
Brito, Bernardo de 9
bulls and bullfighting 29, 123, 126, 128; *see also* hunting
cane games 39, 51, 101, 121, 132–33, 147; *see also* sports
Cartagena, Alonso de 5, 35 fn. 67, 47 fn. 1, 49 fn. 4, 98 fn. 5
Cassian, St. John 17, 48 fn. 3, 114
Castile 3, 5
Cavendish, William, duke of Newcastle 33
Ceuta 3, 5
children 84–85, 87, 139
Cicero 47 fn. 1, 49 fn. 4
clothing 51, 64, 72–74, 94, 108, 136, 137, 142
coronel lancehead 36, 37, 38, 122; *see also* lance

Correia da Serra, José 1–2, 11
curb 23, 24, 111, 112, 151, 152
deer 132
depression 4–5, 66
dogs 79, 127, 129
Duarte I
    administration 5, 6, 68
    biography 3–6, 12, 42–43, 145
    writings 8, 48–49
Eleanor of Aragon 6, 7, 9, 11
England 3, 60, 62
equestrian literature 2, 13–17, 23, 34
falconry 49, 85, 101, 107, 135, 136
Fernando, Infante of Portugal 3, 6
France 1, 11, 62
gaits 29–30, 61, 65, 103
Giles of Rome 8, 17, 136, 138 fn. 30
girth 18, 19, 26, 72, 111, 152, 153
grapper 30, 31, 105, 110
Grisone, Federico 2, 14, 23 n. 47, 33
hackamore 25, 110
hackney 17, 84
helm 31, 36, 37, 108, 109, 121; *see also* armor
horses
    breeding 51, 52, 56
    classification 17–18
    psychology 32–34
    training 51, 52, 56, 58, 150
    vices 63–64, 67, 72, 84–85, 145–46, 150, 153–54
    see also hackney; mule; veterinary medicine
hunting 7, 29, 34, 39, 49, 52, 85, 101, 123–29, 132, 134, 135, 147, 149
injuries 104, 131, 135, 143
Ireland 3, 29, 148
Italy 1, 60; *see also* Sicily

javelin 1, 39, 132
jennet riding and equipment 7, 21–22, 27–29, 61, 71, 73; *see also* brida riding; saddle; spurs
João I 3, 5, 6, 7–8, 34, 49 fn. 6, 70, 127, 135, 136, 138, 143
Jordanus Ruffus 2
jousting 20, 35–38, 51, 60, 68, 69, 104–13, 119–23, 146
   straps used in 21, 69, 107, 110
   see also lance; tourneying
Julius Caesar 48
jumping 61, 63, 84, 147
lance 27, 28, 30–32, 36, 37, 38, 107, 123; *see also* coronel lancehead; jousting; spear
lance-rest 30, 31, 104, 104, 106, 107, 110
latigo 19, 72, 153
Leal Conselheiro 1, 4, 6, 8, 9, 66, 114 fn. 17, 117 fn. 19
Moors 5, 21, 27–29, 39, 62, 148
Monte, Pietro 14, 15 n. 33, 16, 21 n. 43, 35, 36 n. 71, 39, 40–41, 43, 49 fn. 6, 53 fn. 11
mule 84, 154
Nunes de Leão, Duarte 9
pedagogy 16, 84–85, 104–5, 109, 130
Pedro, Infante of Portugal 3, 8, 49 fn. 4, 138 fn. 30
Philippa of Lancaster 3, 138
Pina, Rui de 7, 8, 9
pouch for jousting lance 32, 103
reins 22–23, 25, 65, 100, 110, 111–13, 125, 152
   running reins 26, 111–13
rod 57, 64, 150–51; *see also* whip
saddle 7, 18–22, 28, 31, 37, 50, 58, 59–63, 68–72, 76; *see also* arções
   Brabant saddle 20, 26, 31, 59–60, 61, 62, 68, 69, 73
   French saddle 11, 28, 71, 148
   iron strut on 20, 21, 64
   jennet saddle 7, 21–22, 61, 62, 68, 69, 76, 131

jousting saddle 20–21, 37, 60, 110
pack-saddle 19, 62
see also arções
saddle-cover 20, 71, 153
saddle-flaps 20, 71
saddle-tree 18, 19, 71
shield 37, 108, 109, 110, 122; *see also* adarga
Sicily 18, 148
soltura (fluidity) 13, 15, 16, 42, 57, 98
spear 28, 29, 30, 39, 41, 51, 63, 74–75, 77, 101–11, 123–32, 135; *see also* lance; throwing
sports 35, 53, 134, 137; *see also* cane games; jousting; throwing; tourneying; vaulting
spurs 26–27, 31, 57, 73, 94, 97, 106–7, 110, 131, 145–51, 153
   jennet spurs 26, 149
   rowel spurs 26, 27, 148, 149, 153
stirrups 19–20, 22, 28, 59–62, 68, 70–71, 97, 123, 152–53
   bound 21 fn. 43, 22, 60, 76
   covered stirrups 22, 71
stirrup-leathers 19, 20, 70–71, 97
sword 41–43, 63, 74–75, 77, 101, 133–35
tack *see* bridle; girth; saddle; spurs; stirrups
Tangier 6
throwing 29, 39, 40, 51, 53, 63, 75, 77, 85, 101, 130–33, 135, 147; *see also* cane-games
tilt 37–38, 111, 113, 122–23
tourneying 36, 51, 60, 133–34; *see also* jousting
vamplate 36, 37, 104, 110
vaulting 39–40, 135–36
Vegetius 8, 17, 39, 136 fn. 28, 138
veterinary medicine 34, 56, 58
warfare 43, 50, 51
whip 150; *see also* rod
wrestling 7, 42, 45, 76–77, 121, 139–44
Xenophon 2, 13

Armour and Weapons

I.
The Artillery of the Dukes of Burgundy, 1363–1477
Robert Douglas Smith and Kelly DeVries

II.
'The Furie of the Ordnance': Artillery in the English Civil Wars
Stephen Bull

III.
Jousting in Medieval and Renaissance Iberia
Noel Fallows

IV.
The Art of Swordsmanship by Hans Lecküchner
translated by Jeffrey L. Forgeng

V.
The Book of Horsemanship by Duarte I of Portugal
translated by Jeffrey L. Forgeng

VI.
Pietro Monte's Collectanea:
The Arms, Armour and Fighting Techniques
of a Fifteenth-Century Soldier
translated by Jeffrey L. Forgeng

VII.
The Medieval Military Engineer:
From the Roman Empire to the Sixteenth Century
Peter Purton

VIII.
Royal and Urban Gunpowder Weapons in Late Medieval England
Dan Spencer

IX.
The Sword: Form and Thought
edited by Lisa Deutscher, Mirjam Kaiser and Sixt Wetzler

X.
*Medieval Arms and Armour: a Sourcebook. Volume I:
The Fourteenth Century*
Ralph Moffat

XI.
A Cultural History of the Medieval Sword: Power, Piety and Play
Robert W. Jones

XII.
*The Thun-Hohenstein Album:
Cultures of Remembrance in a Paper Armory*
Chassica Kirchhoff

www.ingramcontent.com/pod-product-compliance
Lightning Source LLC
Chambersburg PA
CBHW071205240426
43668CB00032B/2101